Engine No 2931 Arlington Court *positioned on the stationary test plant in Swindon Works* (British Railways).

CLASSIC LOCOMOTIVES
GREAT WESTERN 'SAINT' CLASS 4-6-0
O.S.Nock

PSL Patrick Stephens, Cambridge

First published in 1983

British Library Cataloguing in Publication Data

Nock, O.S.
  The Great Western 'Saint' Class 4-6-0.—(Classic British locomotives)
  1. Great Western Railway—History
  2. Locomotives—England—History—20th century
  I. Title   II. Series
  625.2'61'0942   TJ603.G72G7

  ISBN 0-85059-632-7

Photoset in 10 pt Plantin by Manuset Limited, Baldock, Herts. Printed in Great Britain on 115 gsm Fineblade coated cartridge, and bound, by William Clowes Limited, Beccles, Suffolk, for the publishers, Patrick Stephens Limited, Bar Hill, Cambridge, CB3 8EL, England.

Contents

Above *Engine No 6813* Eastbury Grange *on the Plymouth–Manchester express climbing Hemerdon bank* (the late M.W. Earley).

Below *Engine No 2903* Lady of Lyons *as running in 1948, in plain green, but just after nationalisation with no railway name, or crest on tender.*

Preface

To name the greatest-ever steam locomotive in British practice would seem the surest way to start a controversy that would rage for months in the correspondence columns of every enthusiast journal. But on the grounds of longevity, and capacity for maximum output in relation to nominal tractive powers, the Great Western 'Saints' must be very nearly second to none, if not entirely without rivals. In this book, the evolution of their design is analysed, and details of running achievements recorded that are not only thrilling in themselves, but which, in relation to the size, weight, and nominal power of the locomotives, stand alone in my personal experience.

From the viewpoint of locomotive history it is a pity that nearly all these exceptional performances took place after the 'Saints' had passed beyond the stage of close scrutiny by indicating and dynamometer car testing, and that efforts of comparable merit had not been documented in the completeness we should now require to place them on the pinnacle which all the available evidence indicates that they deserve. Two instances only need to be mentioned at this stage: an *attained* speed of 31 mph on a gradient of 1 in 95, with a 450 ton load, and an *attained* 64½ mph on a gradient of 1 in 254 with a load of 320 tons, requiring outputs of 1300 and 1400 equivalent drawbar horsepower, respectively.

The data on which the purely technical aspects of train running are based was published at various times in railway and engineering journals prior to 1925, but more recently I have been very fortunate in having the records of the Rev W.A. Dunn, made available to me by his son, and the invaluable notebooks compiled by the late A.V. Goodyear, whose experience of Great Western running extended back to 1904. My grateful thanks are also due to the locomotive authorities at Swindon Works, for allowing me to peruse old records, and particularly the dynamometer car rolls.

O.S. Nock
Bath, March 1983

Overleaf *Swindon Works 'A' erecting shop showing, on left, 'Star' Class 4-6-0 No 4035* Queen Charlotte *and on right the 'Saint' Class 4-6-0 No 2948* Stackpole Court *under major repair* (British Railways).
Below *One of the derivatives: 'Hall' Class 4-6-0 No 5978* Bodininick Hall *on the Wolverhampton–Paignton express near Flax Bourton* (C.R.L. Coles).

Chapter 1

New century—new outlook

In the last decade of the nineteenth century the locomotive department of the Great Western Railway was weathering the great upheaval of the final abolition of the broad gauge. For a few years at any rate there were few signs of how the company was going to face up to the challenge of the new era, of an all standard gauge railway. When *The Railway Magazine* was first launched, in July 1897, on page 1 of volume 1 there began an illustrated interview with the General Manager of the GWR, Mr J.L. (afterwards Sir Joseph) Wilkinson, and he spoke of the new routes, and short cuts that had already been authorised, but the Dean 7 ft 8 in, 4-2-2 'singles' were still the premier express passenger locomotives. It is true that the 'Badminton' Class of 4-4-0 was to come out at the very end of that same year, but these did not in any way replace the beautiful 4-2-2 singles. In the previous year, however, G.J. Churchward had been appointed Locomotive Works Manager at Swindon, and from that time onwards he gradually assumed the role of the 'power behind the throne'. Henceforth Great Western locomotives began, little by little, to partake of a 'new look'.

The top management of the GWR was developing a new outlook on passenger traffic policy, going all-out to foster holiday traffic not only to the growing resorts of South Devon and Cornwall, but also to South and West Wales. The genial and equable climates suggested that this traffic should not be confined to the traditional summer seasons, but prolonged even to the extent of encouraging winter visiting. At the same time, there were attractive possibilities in promoting prestige ocean traffic at Plymouth, and in the tourist business to and from the South of Ireland, to which the GWR already provided the fastest service from London. While the speeding up of passenger trains had received something of a jolt in 1896 following the alarming wreck of the sharply-timed West Coast 'Tourist' express at Preston, the travelling public appreciated the running of trains making long non-stop runs, because of the comfort and undisturbed journeys that resulted. Although the accident at Preston had put something of a damper on acceleration prospects in general it was known in railway circles that the derailment, fortunately attended by minimal loss of life, was the result of gross mismanagement, so far as locomotive personnel was concerned.

The priority the locomotive department of the Great Western Railway faced in 1898-9 was the need to provide power for many more lengthy non-stop runs, and for the conveyance of much heavier loads. At that time there was no thought of such modern phenomena as fixed formation trains, as exemplified by the modern HSTs. Locomotive power, as it was seen at the turn of the century, had to be adequate to cope with the month to month, or even day to day fluctuation in the volume of passenger traffic. In the early 1900s the Great Western came to advertising itself as 'The Holiday Line', and that, of course, was just asking for wide fluctuations in traffic density.

Churchward more than once publicly expressed the view that the principal problem in locomotive development was that of the boiler, and in tracing the history of constructional work at Swindon from 1898 onwards it can be seen how the design process was guided from the Dean 'singles' to the full flowering of the express passenger 4-6-0s of 1906-1911. The occasions on which the full capacity of these large locomotives was needed were then few and far between, but from the first innovations which he got incorporated into what were basically Dean designs, Churchward very carefully paved his way.

The essential need was for new locomotives which would not only have a very high maximum power output, with good economy, but which would be equally efficient when lightly worked. Though it was not generally appreciated at the time, he was helped by the fundamental characteristics of the steam locomotive, which, unlike the diesel, maintains its efficiency over a wide range of power output. Of course, the overall efficiency of the diesel is very much higher than that of steam, but the ideal method of working the former is to keep as near as possible to full capacity for most of the time. In the ideas he put forward for trial while Dean was still in the chair at Swindon there is ample evidence that he was looking at the all-round efficiency of operation—not merely the attainment of high power output and high speed, but economy in maintenance

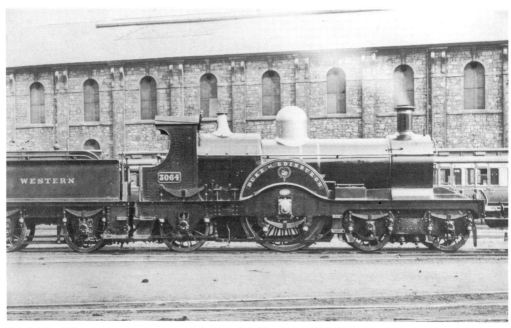

The height of 19th century elegance—one of the Dean 7 ft 8 in singles, No 3064 Duke of Edinburgh *(P.J.T. Reed).*

charges and simplicity in basic design, and since the boiler was potentially the most expensive part of the locomotive to maintain, it was that which received his first attention.

In his beautiful 7 ft 8 in bogie 'singles' William Dean had revived an important and commendable feature of Daniel Gooch's design practice, in raising the firebox above the level of the boiler and thus providing increased steam space in the hottest area. In the 'Badminton' Class 4-4-0s, of which the first was completed at Swindon just at the close of 1897, this feature was developed by use of the Belpaire type of firebox, again with its top raised considerably above the line of the boiler. This provided a notable increase in the area at the waterline, and was instrumental in reducing foaming in the boiler at times of maximum steam production. This feature of the 'Badmintons', prominent externally, did not please those who set store on the artistry of locomotive lineaments.

A correspondent writing in *The Railway Magazine* for October 1899, prefaced an account of some good runs with the new engines with the following remarks: 'A very large Belpaire firebox hardly improves the appearance of the engine, but gives ample grate area. The overhung springs and extended smokebox are far from pleasing features in the design, and here they are particularly aggressive. It is a curious anomaly that a line which possesses in its "singles" some of the handsomest engines in the world should produce coupled engines which can hardly be termed other than hideous'!

Incidentally, the grate area of the 'Badmintons' was *less* than that of the 7 ft 8 in bogie singles, 18.3 sq ft, against 20.8 sq ft. Both classes were alike, however, in having a large and spectacular dome, polished brass, and the keeping of this in spotless condition was a task in which the shed staff took especial pride. Although at that time the Great Western possessed a number of engines with domeless boilers it was generally thought desirable to provide a large dome in which the steam collected and to locate the regulator in the dome. By this priming, or the passing of water direct from the boiler to the cylinders, would be minimised—or so it was thought. But the provision of a dome, especially one so large as that used on the 'Badmintons', needed an equally large hole in the boiler itself, and that, of course, was a point of weakness in the boiler construction, and one likely to induce problems in maintenance. On Churchward's recommendation, one of the 'Badmintons', engine No 3310, *Waterford*, was built with a domeless boiler, with the safety valves mounted in a brass casing shaped rather like a truncated milk churn. Thus, one of the most uniquely characteristic features of many thousands of later Great Western locomotives originated.

It is very amusing to read some contemporary comments on this feature of the design. *The Railway Magazine* was then feeling its way with some of the earliest lithographed colour plates—very crude they seem, nowadays! In its issue of February 1900, *Waterford* was so depicted, with the following comments: 'The principal feature of this engine is its immense boiler, which is so high pitched that with the vehicular loading gauge obtaining on British railways, no space remains for a dome or for a safety valve in its usual position on the firebox. Mr Dean has, therefore, placed the safety valve of *Waterford* in the position on the boiler barrel usually occupied by the steam dome. The centre of the boiler is 8 ft 6 in above rail level, necessitating the employment of a small funnel, the top of which is 13 ft 1½ in above the rails.'

But while *Waterford* had the same sized cylinders as the rest of the 'Badminton' Class, the boiler certainly was much larger, with a total heating surface of 1520.03 sq ft, against 1296.60, and a grate area of 23.65 sq ft against 18.32 sq ft. Those whose appraisal of locomotive design was based upon aesthetic or artistic grounds, and who had apostrophised the 'Badmintons' as hideous, were in for some further shocks in April 1900 when the first of the 'Atbara' Class 4-4-0s was completed at Swindon; for in them not only were the extended smokebox and high raised Belpaire firebox perpetuated, but the flowing curves of the running plate in the earliest engines were replaced by the stark simplicity of square cut outside frames, carried well forward of the leading coupled wheels. The gorgeous colouring of old remained, but from whatever angle one regarded them the 'Atbaras' were not very handsome locomotives.

The 20 engines of the 'Atbara' Class were completed at Swindon between April and September 1900, and, proving very successful in traffic, they were followed by a further 20, turned out in June-October 1901. By that time Dean's health was failing, and with the full approbation of the directors, the responsibility for day to day management of the locomotive department was falling upon Churchward's shoulders. It was done with consummate tact. Nothing was done that would give Dean any idea that he was not still in full charge, and the changes in design and outward appearance of the locomotives were credited to him, and him alone, though they were due almost entirely to Churchward. Everyone on the GWR had a great affection for Dean, and the steps by which the transition was effected were always of the kindest.

Nothing of what was happening within the shrouded walls of Swindon Works was evident in contemporary descriptions of the new locomotives. Among the engineering *littérateurs* of the day, Charles Rous-Marten had his ear very close to the ground, but if he knew, or suspected what was afoot, he certainly made not a whisper of it when he went to almost inordinate length in discussing the great event of March 1902, in *The Railway Magazine*. This was the completion of the first Great Western express passenger 4-6-0, No 100, and in quoting extensively from his article, in the following month, I hope to show something of the *impressement* which the event created in his vividly active mind.

Smaller wheeled 4-4-0 for the South Devon and Cornish banks: No 3252 Duke of Cornwall (British Railways).

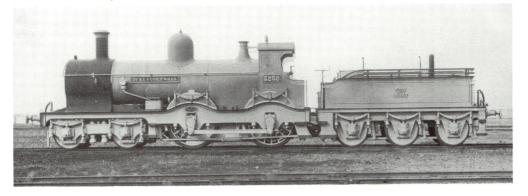

The first of the 'Badminton' Class, express passenger 4-4-0, with high raised Belpaire firebox, built in Swindon in 1897 (British Railways).

'The event of the past month in respect of British locomotive practice' he wrote 'is Mr W. Dean's enlistment of the Great Western Railway in the small and select corps of British railways that use six-coupled express engines. The latest locomotive designed by him and turned out early in March from the Swindon Works forms the third British instance of this arrangement being adopted for express service.'

After referring to other British 4-6-0s he continued: 'The new Great Western engine, the latest product of Mr Dean's mechanical genius is intended, I understand, for use on the steep grades of Devon and Cornwall, which are as steep as 1 in 55 to 1 in 60 for many miles together both ways, whilst at some points on the Dartmoor, Rattery, and Hemerdon banks even rise at 1 in 43, 1 in 41, and 1 in 40. I am not aware that express trains having an inclusive speed of over 40 miles an hour are run anywhere in the world over gradients so severe as these. Yet the Great Western Railway accomplishes the feat, and does it in good style, too, with its 5 ft 8 in, four-coupled bogie engines of the domeless "Camel" or "Avalon" type, which have cylinders 18 in by 26 in, as it did with their similarly-dimensioned but smaller-boilered predecessors *Duke of Cornwall, Pendennis Castle*, and the rest of the class. Only with loads of 200 tons and upward, which are of daily occurrence during the summer months, recourse was compulsorily had to pilot assistance.'

Then, after some remarks about piloting generally, Rous-Marten developed his main

discussion of the new engines, particularly in respect of the unusually long piston stroke of 30 in. He continued: 'It is the special difficulty of the Great Western Railway that its worst banks do not lie within compact limits, like that of the London and North-Western Railway at Shap, or those of the Caledonian at Beattock and Dunblane, which can be conveniently worked with the aid of a bank engine stationed at the foot. From Newton Abbot to Penzance, a distance of 112½ miles, there is hardly a single level stretch of any material length. Putting aside the relatively easy bit across the tableland extending between the Rattery and Hemerdon summits, about 12 miles, the road is a series of perpetually recurrent steep-sided gables, far severer than the Shap, Beattock, Dunblane, Falahill, Whitrope, or Barrhead incline, or than the grades by which the London and South-Western crosses Dartmoor; worse even, on the average, than those of the Aviemore-Culloden cut on the Highland line. Such conditions manifestly demanded "heroic" treatment. Obviously this is how Mr Dean has viewed the case, for he has produced a novel type of locomotive that ought exactly to fulfil the requirements indicated. With a vast boiler 5 ft in diameter, and a huge Belpaire firebox more than 9 ft, in length, 2,400 square feet of heating surface, cylinders 18 in by 30 in six-coupled 6 ft 8 in wheels, some 50 tons of adhesion weight, and a steam pressure of 200 lbs, per square inch, the new locomotive necessarily possesses immense nominal strength, which she should be able to develop fully in actual practice. Thus the newest Great

A 'Badminton' with a domeless boiler: No 3310 Waterford, *a prototype in GWR boiler design* (British Railways).

Western engine must be classed as one of the most powerful ever yet placed on British metals for passenger express duty, as it is much the heaviest, weighing as it does no less than 69 tons without the tender.

'It may be observed that in his newest locomotive Mr Dean has departed strikingly (1) from the special traditions of his railway in one important respect, viz, in using outside instead of inside cylinders; (2) from British traditions generally in employing so great a length of piston stroke as 30 inches.

'The former plan is, of course, no novelty outside the Great Western, even for six-coupled engines, there being many old locomotives of this type on the Caledonian line, built for mineral traffic, while the newer six-coupled express engines of the North-Eastern and Highland lines both have outside cylinders. But their employment on the Great Western under the present conditions is quite a fresh departure. It affords another illustration of a fact to which I have more than once called attention—that whenever a particular method appears on the eve of becoming utterly extinct in British locomotive practice, something invariably occurs which gives it a new lease of life.

'Time after time outside cylinders have seemed to be on the extreme verge of extinction on British railways, and then something has always happened to save them. The cases of the London and South-Western with its four-cylinder non-compound, of the Great Northern with its "990" Class, of the London and North-Western with its compounds, of the Midland and North-Eastern with their newest compounds, and of

the North-Eastern and Highland with their six-coupled express type, will at once suggest themselves. And now the Great Western affords a fresh instance. Mr Dean no doubt would, as usual, have placed his cylinders inside the frames could he have found room for them. But this is not easy with six-coupled wheels of large diameter, while with a piston stroke so long as 30 in, owing to the length of the crank-throw, it would probably be quite impracticable.

'Although the point does not necessarily arise in the present connection, it may be worthwhile to observe that those people who regard the old broad-gauge as a mistake, a mere fad of an ambitious engineer, and who declare our standard 4 ft 8½ in, gauge equal to all requirements, must begin to realise the serious restrictions which the narrower width and the lowness of our load-gauge vertical limit impose in respect of increased power. If you desire a fairly large driving wheel, you must curtail your length of stroke, else you will raise your boiler so high that the chimney will be knocked down by the first bridge or tunnel. If you desire big cylinders you cannot conveniently or satisfactorily get them inside the frames owing to the narrowness of the available space. If you therefore compulsorily place them outside, then you must "mind your eye" and not make them too large, or they will strip off the edge of the first station platform you come to, or cut a groove in the side of the next tunnel. These would be awkward incidents, and are wisely avoided by our locomotive designers. But the necessity of avoidance imposes much otherwise unnecessary planning and scheming.

'Now, Mr Dean in his new engine has adhered to the cylinder diameter which has given him such excellent results in the "Atbaras", "Badmintons", "Cornwalls", and "Camels" *viz* 18 in, manifestly he finds that the boiler pressure of 180 lbs to 200 lbs, of steam with the relative pressure on the piston area which an 18 in diameter yields, *viz* about 255 square inches, provides an initial motive force ample for his requirements. And so instead of employing cylinders 20 in in diameter, as he did originally in the 7 ft 8 in singles and in the 7 ft coupled "Armstrongs" with a 24 in piston stroke in the former case and a 26 in stroke in the latter, he has determined to obtain enhanced effective power by multiplying that initial force through the aid of leverage. This was the principle upon which the late Mr Patrick Stirling proceeded when he designed his celebrated 8 ft single wheelers. He gave them a stroke of no less than 28 in, in order to secure augmented haulage power, while the large wheel-diameter allowed a slower movement of the reciprocating and revolving parts at a given speed.

'But Mr Dean has "gone one better" than this. By adopting a stroke of no less than 30 in in length, he has taken a virtually new departure in British locomotive practice. So far as I am aware, this extraordinary length of stroke has only once before been tried in Great Britain for express work at any rate. That was in the case of a batch of 7 ft coupled express engines designed by Mr W. Bouch, which came into the hands of the North-Eastern Railway on the absorption of one of the numerous smaller lines which are now incorporated in its vast system. These engines, which were numbered 1268, 1269, 1270 etc, had leading bogies and 17 in, outside cylinders, with a 30 in, piston stroke. They were built many years ago, and were reported to have done good work. Those were the only British express engines that I know of which ever had a 30 in, stroke, and, as it will be noticed, the peculiarity was not perpetuated, nor has it been revived in this country—although the case is otherwise in America—until this new departure on the part of Mr Dean on the Great Western Railway.

'As to the advantages and disadvantages of a long piston stroke, I have had something to say in earlier articles of this series. The question is one upon which the highest authorities differ *toto cælo*. Mr Dean himself long maintained a maximum limit of 24 in, for all his passenger engines excepting the few employed on the South Devon and Cornwall lines. To them he gave 26 in, as he did also to his four 7 ft coupled of the "Armstrong" Class, and subsequently to his "Cornwalls", "Camels", "Badmintons", and "Atbaras". Messrs D. and P. Drummond, Billinton, Kirtley, J. Stirling, Wainright, Johnson, W. Worsdell, Robinson, Aspinall, Holmes, Manson, and M'Intosh, all hold by a 26 in

stroke. So does Mr Ivatt in his numerous "400" and "1321" Classes, his twelve single wheelers, and his goods engines, but he prefers 24 in in his "990" or Atlantic type. Mr Holden long kept to a 24 in stroke, but latterly has substituted 26 in, and has also lengthened the stroke of some of the 24 in engines to 25 in. Mr Webb has always consistently and persistently adhered to 24 in. Both the 8 ft single wheelers and the large mineral traffic engines built by the late Mr Patrick Stirling for the Great Northern had 28 in stroke. The French express engines on M de Glehn's four cylinder compound principle, which are now the standard type on all the main lines in France, have uniformly a 25¼ in, piston stroke. Some American engines have 28 in, 30 in, and even 32 in, stroke.

'Thus "doctors differ" so widely that it would be presumptuous for an outside engineer to "lay down the law" on such a point. It will be manifest to everybody possessing even the most rudimentary acquaintance with mechanical engineering that a long stroke has the advantage of increasing by leverage the practical efficiency of the motive force supplied by the steam pressure on the pistons, and that it has the disadvantage—

if that be really a disadvantage, which is much disputed—of proportionately accelerating the piston speed, because the piston has so much longer distance to travel in the given time of each stroke. Every locomotive engineer has to weigh the one thing against the other, and then to judge which, in his particular circumstances, must be allowed to send down the scale. Probably in most instances where the highest speeds have to be run on a road of moderate difficulty, the shorter stroke of 24 in to 26 in, will be preferred as affording a lower piston speed. But when very heavy loads have to be hauled over severe gradients, especially when the descents are too steep or curved to

Left *The high raised Belpaire firebox applied to a 4-2-2 single: No 3027* Worcester *(British Railways).*
Above *No more flowing curves in the frames: one of the 'Atbara' Class 4-4-0s, built in Swindon in 1898, No 3375* Edgcumbe *(British Railways).*
Right *The new chief: G.J. Churchward, at the time of his appointment as Locomotive, Carriage & Wagon Superintendent, in 1902 (British Railways).*

The first GWR express passenger 4-6-0, No 100 (British Railways).

warrant extreme downhill velocities, then the extra long stroke, such as 28 in or 30 in, can undoubtedly be employed with great advantage on the score of increment of power, thus often obviating the use of a pilot engine. Mr Dean's new experiment will be watched with deep interest by all locomotive engineers.'

From whom Rous-Marten got the idea that the new engine was to work *west* of Newton Abbot we are not to know, but we do know that as early as 1901 Churchward had in mind a 5 ft 8 in 4-6-0 for use in the West Country.

So far as the last years of Dean's career were concerned, the principal difficulty was that his memory was failing and that the directors found it impossible to transact any business with him. Yet the new developments were introduced in such a way as to convince Dean that he was solely responsible for them. By the early summer of 1902, although he was then no more than 62 years of age, he was by the kindest of suggestions prevailed upon to retire. The company found a quiet retreat for him at Folkestone, and before his leaving, his fellow officers entertained him to a sumptuous dinner at the Trocadero Restaurant in London. It was a characteristic gesture on the part of those who organised it to put a photograph of the 4-6-0 engine No 100 on the cover of the menu card, as representing the culminating event of his career, whereas in fact Churchward was entirely responsible for that engine. It was subsequently named *William Dean*.

Chapter 2

4-6-0s: The boiler and the engine

The design of the first three express passenger 4-6-0s of the Great Western Railway provides an absorbing study, on two quite distinct yet closely interrelated fields. The boilers of the 'Atbara' Class 4-4-0s had steamed freely, and in designing the pioneer express 4-6-0 the much larger boiler needed was a straight enlargement of the 'Atbara'. It had the same type of high raised Belpaire firebox, and a barrel that was larger in diameter, longer, but entirely parallel. The comparative dimensions were:

Engine class	'Atbara'	No 100
Length of barrel (ft-in)	11 - 0	14 - 8
Diameter (ft-in)	4 - 5	5 - 0
Firebox-length (ft-in)	7 - 0	9 - 0
Grate area (sq ft)	21.28	27¾
Total heating surface (sq ft)	1,664.28	2,400
Pressure (lb/sq in)	180	200

The tube heating surface of the 'Atbaras' was provided by 277 tubes of $1\frac{7}{8}$ in, outside diameter, and with a distance between the tube plates of 11 ft $3\frac{13}{16}$ in, gave a heating surface of 1540.18 sq ft. The larger diameter of the boiler of the 4-6-0 engine enabled 300 tubes to be accommodated, and brought the tube heating surface up to 2252.94 sq ft.

So far as the engine proper was concerned, Rous-Marten in his lengthy dissertation about the cylinder proportions seems to have missed the point over Churchward's use of a 30 in stroke, and he made no reference to the special constructional feature of the front end. The cylinders, together with their associated piston valves, were made in two identical castings each with a half-saddle, and bolted together on the engine centre line. This allows for easily arranged exhaust passages, which were simplified to obviate the need for separate exhaust piping and numerous joints, all of which would have to have been made steam tight.

Some years later, Churchward, questioned as to why he had adopted the long piston stroke of 30 in, said it was the only way he knew of making a simple engine equal to a compound, in thermal efficiency. From this it would seem that he saw the challenge of the compound locomotive some little time before the importing of the De Glehn 'Atlantics'. The piston valves were of the double-ported type of 6½ in, diameter, actuated by Stephenson's link motion through an arrangement of rocking levers as shown in the accompanying drawing. This particular design was used only on engine No 100, and it did not provide the valve setting that afterwards became such an important feature of Great Western two-cylinder locomotives.

At the time of the construction of engine No 100, James Inglis was Chief Engineer, and at first he had some doubts about the use of the engine into Paddington. This was not permitted until some tests had been made on the viaduct over the Uxbridge Road, near Hanwell. Certainly, in 1902, the engine was working principally between Bristol and

The second express passenger 4-6-0 No 98, photographed at Laira sheds, Plymouth, showing the short-cone type of taper boiler (P.J.T. Reed).

Newton Abbot, a regular turn being the overnight North to West mail leaving Temple Meads at 6.15 am. This was quite a heavy train, though not one likely to overtax the abilities of such a powerful new engine. From 1904, when the Cornish Riviera Express was first put on, running non-stop between Paddington and Plymouth, via Bristol, No 100 took her turn on this 'star' train. The expert speed recorder of those days, the Rev W.J. Scott, logged an excellent run on the eastbound 'non-stop', when a late start of 8 min from Plymouth was converted into an on time arrival in Paddington, and had the engine not been markedly eased down after passing Slough the arrival could have been several minutes early. The accompanying log of the journey shows some interesting features. The hill climbing, even with so relatively light a load as 175 tons, was not very good, and in fact time was lost between Exeter and Wellington, and again between Bath and Chippenham. On the other hand the engine ran freely on the level and favourable stretches. Scott went into raptures over it, though on a contemporary run one of the 4-4-0s made even faster running.

The Cornish Riviera Express in 1904

Load: 7 coaches 175 tons. Engine No 100 *William Dean.*

Distance miles	Schedule min	Actual m s	Average speed mph
0.0 PLYMOUTH			
(North Rd)	0	0 00	—
4.0 Plympton		6 22	37.7
6.7 *Hemerdon Box*	11	11 48	29.8
14.1 Wrangaton		21 20	46.7
		pw slack	
23.1 Totnes	32	31 36	52.8
27.9 *Dainton Box*		39 03	38.7
31.8 NEWTON ABBOT	44½	44 56	39.8
37.0 Teignmouth		51 47	45.6
52.0 EXETER	70	70 35	47.6
66.9 Tiverton Junction		88 13	50.6
71.9 *Whiteball Box*		94 00	51.9
75.7 Wellington	94	97 37	63.1
82.8 TAUNTON	101	103 06	77.1
88.6 Durston		107 45	74.6
94.3 Bridgwater		112 40	68.8
107.9 *Uphill Junction*	124	124 55	66.6
115.6 Yatton		131 25	71.0
126.9 *Pylle Hill Junction*	143	142 50	59.4
128.6 *Bristol East Depot*		146 40	27.8
138.7 BATH	158	157 55	53.8
146.6 *Box Tunnel East*		167 37	49.1
151.6 Chippenham	172	172 57	56.2
157.9 Dauntsey		178 02	74.2
162.7 Wootton Bassett		182 35	63.5
168.3 SWINDON	189	187 46	64.8
192.5 DIDCOT	212	207 27	73.8
209.6 READING	229	222 17	69.3
214.6 Twyford		226 50	66.0
221.4 Maidenhead		232 52	68.0
227.1 SLOUGH	245	238.00 eased	66.5
239.9 Ealing Broadway		249 50	41.6
245.6 PADDINGTON	265	257 00	—

The differences between No 100 and the second express passenger 4-6-0 were profound. The evolution of the tapered boiler barrel had begun even while No 100 was making her early trial runs, and the first engine to have the form of boiler that was to become historic was one of the double-framed inside-cylinder 2-6-0s of the 'Aberdare' Class, No 2662. This was quickly followed by its application to an 'Atbara', No 3405 *Mauritius.* The design was not quite finalised on these two locomotives, for while they had the tapered barrel, the firebox was straight sided in its upper half and the curves at the top were relatively sharp, as in the 'Atbaras' and the 5 ft 8 in 'Camel' Class 4-4-0s. The top surface of the firebox, also, was horizontal.

When Churchward came to apply the same principles of design to the 4-6-0 locomotive No 98, built at Swindon in 1903, there was a notable difference from the 4-4-0s in respect of the tube sizes, for while in developing the standard No 4 taper boiler from that of the 'Atbara' he used 350 tubes of $1\frac{5}{8}$ in outside diameter, against 277 tubes of $1\frac{7}{8}$ in diameter for the 'Atbara' in No 98 he increased the tube size to 2 in, and used only 250 tubes. This would seem a logical step in view of the greater length between the tube plates, and it proved so absolutely right in practice that it became the standard dimension for the No 1 boiler, continued when superheating was applied, and in all subsequent classes of locomotive carrying the same standard boiler.

The idea behind the taper boiler, which was derived directly from contemporary American practice, was to obtain free circulation of the water in the hottest part of the boiler and to avoid the abrupt transition in cross-sectional area from the square-sided Belpaire firebox of No 100 to the parallel 5 ft diameter of the barrel. The firebox on the No 98 was tapered

An early 'snap' of No 100 on an eastbound train, leaving Bath, while the engine still retained the parallel domeless boiler (W.A. Dunn).

towards the back, both at the sides and on top, to give increased space all round at the forward end. Churchward spent a great deal of time personally on the development of the curvature of the side plates of the firebox, not only to secure the good circulation he considered essential, but also to ensure minimum stay stresses from the relative expansions of the firebox and the casings. Direct staying for all surfaces was employed. The standard No 1 boiler bore an almost uncanny likeness to one introduced on the Illinois Central Railroad in 1897, in all the finer points of its detail, except that the American used a steam dome on the tapered rearward portion of the barrel. The drawing office records at Swindon show that the American drawing was booked in on August 19 1902, when the design of the standard No 1 was being finalised. The firebox of the Illinois Central boiler was 9 ft 9 in long, and the barrel 13 ft long. The grate area was 27.18 sq ft, almost exactly the same as the Great Western's.

It has often been said that Churchward's genius lay not in the field of original design but in his ability to recognise a good thing when he saw it, and in skilful adaptation to his own needs. The way in which one line of American boiler practice was adapted was perhaps the most striking instance of all.

The Illinois Central was far from characteristic of the general trend of North American practice. There, the wide firebox with very large grate areas was being adopted, largely to cope with low grade coal, but Churchward set his face against this trend, one reason being because of the standardisation programme he had already determined upon. The large No 1 boiler was to be used not only on the 6 ft 8 in, 4-6-0 express type, but on its 5 ft 8 in, counterpart, and on the 2-8-0 heavy mineral engine. The intermittent demands for steam on the average English heavy goods run, and the amount of time standing, would result in serious stand-by losses in a locomotive with a large grate in the American style, simply from the need to keep the firebars covered. The narrow grate was also very suitable for burning soft Welsh coal, generally used on the Great Western. Furthermore, American engineers themselves were agreed that the Belpaire type of firebox had the advantage of parallel stays in both directions, which made it possible to calculate stresses more accurately, though for them it had the disadvantage of greater weight. The Illinois Central continued to use the Belpaire, with deep narrow grates, even up to a very powerful 4-8-0 freighter of 1899, with a tractive effort of 49,700 lb, and a grate area of 37.5 sq ft. The shaping of the firebox is

precisely that which Churchward so assidu-
ously copied.

The original form of the No 1 standard
boiler had a parallel section at the front, with
the rearward part tapering up nearly to the top
level of the firebox. This form became known
as the 'half cone', to distinguish it from the
'full-cone' that followed. The taper was from
4 ft $10\frac{13}{16}$ in outside, to 5 ft 6 in, and it all took
place on the upper line. The lower outline was
horizontal throughout from front to back. In
the original non-superheated form as fitted to
engine No 98, and many subsequent ones, the
free gas area through the tubes, reckoned as a
percentage of the grate area, was 16 per cent.
This relationship, which is considered to be a
yardstick of boiler performance, was good on
theoretical grounds, and was verified by the
performance of the engine in practice.

The boiler pressure on engine No 98 was
200 lb per sq in, as on No 100. It is an interesting point to speculate upon, whether Churchward would have increased the boiler pressure
in his later 4-6-0s to 225 lb per sq in, without
the French influence, to be discussed later.
His contemporaries on most other British railways took every opportunity that came to
reduce boiler pressure, and so reduce maintenance costs. But he required high sustained
power for the long non-stop runs with the
heavy holiday trains, and reliable steaming on

a minimum of coal consumption. One could
not make long non-stop runs at high speed if
the coal consumption was such as to exhaust
the fireman, or involve carrying a very large
and heavy tender, such as those coming
currently into use on the Caledonian.

Nevertheless, while the boiler was
undoubtedly the principal problem, the front
end was of little less importance, to ensure
that the steam was used economically. The
express locomotives of the Dean era were
notably free running. It was not only the 7 ft
8 in bogie singles. The 'Badminton' Class
4-4-0s ran readily up to 80 mph, and the
'Atbaras' were even faster. Yet they had what
could be called a traditional arrangement of
the Stephenson link motion, with slide valves
having a maximum travel in full gear of $4\frac{5}{8}$ in,
and $\frac{3}{16}$ in 'lead'. This latter quantity is the
amount the valve is open to steam when the
piston itself is at the end of its stroke. By so
setting the valve gear that the valve is open to
steam just *before* the piston reaches the end of
its stroke, some cushioning of the piston is
provided, and a smooth action results. With
the Stephenson link motion, the lead increases
as the gear is linked up, and the cushioning
effect increases at higher speed.

Now at Swindon, at the turn of the century,
there was a senior draughtsman by the name
of W.H. Pearce, who was a specialist on valve

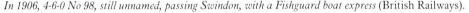

In 1906, 4-6-0 No 98, still unnamed, passing Swindon, with a Fishguard boat express (British Railways).

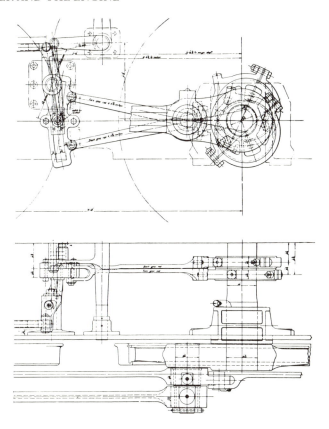

Above *The arrangement of Stephenson's link motion on 4-6-0 No 100, unique on the GWR* (Institution of Mechanical Engineers).

Below *4-6-0 No 98 in early days, leaving Bath with the London-bound express* (W.A. Dunn).

The third 4-6-0, No 171 Albion, *after being converted temporarily to the 'Atlantic' type for comparative tests against the French compounds* (P.J.T. Reed).

gears, and it was on his drawing board that a novel, and then unique arrangement of the Stephenson link motion was developed. Churchward wanted maximum power from his engines, and indicator diagrams taken off some of the newer locomotives showed clearly where power was being lost. It was due to excessive lead.

With the conventional forms of valve gear, whether it be Stephenson's, Joy's, Walschaerts or Allan's, the timing of the valve events are all related. With the 'lead' providing for admission of the steam before the end of the return stroke, the exhaust port closes correspondingly early, and compression begins early. Churchward was convinced that while some cushioning of the pistons was needed when the engine was running at high speed, it was certainly not needed when starting or pounding at slow speed up a heavy gradient, and it was determined that the gear should be designed to provide the minimum lead necessary for cushioning at high speed, no more than $\frac{1}{8}$ in. With the varying lead characteristic of the Stephensons link motion this resulted in there being a *negative* amount of lead in full gear. In other words, the admission valve did not open until the piston had moved $\frac{1}{8}$ in on its forward stroke. This made the point of compression later in the return stroke, and used less power in consequence. Engines with this valve setting were considerably more powerful in getting away with a load than those with a conventional setting and $\frac{1}{8}$ or $\frac{3}{16}$ in positive lead in full gear.

Indicator diagrams taken from earlier engines also showed that a considerable amount of power was being lost through what is termed 'wiredrawing'. In other words, the ports through which the steam entered into

and was exhausted from the cylinders offered some restriction; and this resulted in a drop of steam pressure at inlet, and the setting up of excessive back pressure at exhaust. The port openings could be increased by lengthening what are called the steam 'laps', and lengthening the travel of the valves. At the time many locomotive engineers looked askance at the idea of using long-lap, long-travel valves because it was thought that the longer travels, and consequently higher reciprocating speeds would increase the wear, and add to the maintenance costs. But Churchward felt that the greater power of the locomotives and their greater efficiency due to the improved steam circuit would more than justify the likelihood of greater wear on the moving parts. So engine No 98 had a valve gear providing $5\frac{7}{8}$ in travel in full gear, $1\frac{5}{8}$ in steam lap, and $\frac{1}{8}$ in negative lead in full gear. This increased to $\frac{1}{8}$ in positive lead when the valves were linked up to 25 per cent cut-off. While the cylinders remained the same at 18 in diameter by 30 in stroke, the piston valves were increased from $6\frac{1}{2}$ in to no less than 10 in diameter.

When engine No 98 was completed at Swindon, in March 1903, few of those who looked upon her had any conception of the wellnigh revolutionary features that had been packed into her design. The aesthetes saw only the rather angular profile, and sighed for the flowing curves of the Dean era, while in the rarefied atmosphere of the Institution of Mechanical Engineers, James Stirling, in his retirement, chided Churchward for producing engines that were 'not bonnie'! Actually, compared to some of the creations of more recent times, No 98 had a very neat and compact appearance. The running plate, although cut down square at the front, was continued rearwards in an unbroken line to the cab, and footplate level was attained from the ground by a three-step ladder. The piston valve chests were neatly ensconced beneath the running plate and the cylinder centre line was horizontal, as it was to be in all Churchward's standard locomotives. Solid big-ends contributed to the outward appearance of absence of outside gadgetry. The boiler development had not yet advanced to the stage of extended smokeboxes, and the front coincided harmoniously with the step-down in the running plate.

As on No 100, the cylinders and valve chests on each side of the engine were incorporated in a single casting, following American practice, the two halves, each containing the smokebox saddle, being identical and bolted together on the centre line of the engine. But there was an important difference on No 98, which became thereafter standard practice on all Churchward's two-cylinder engines. The piston valves were much larger, and the depth of the casting below the running plate would not permit of the continuance forward of the plate frames of the locomotives.

American locomotives having the front-end design which had been adopted at Swindon had bar frames, but Churchward did not wish to have a feature so revolutionary in British practice, so an ingenious compromise was worked out, namely that plate frames should be used as far forward as the motion plate, and then forged extension frames were bolted on to produce the equivalent of bar frames at the front end, and enable the combined cylinder, valve chest and smokebox saddle casting to straddle these in true American style. One sensed that the forward extension of these bar frames to the running plate constituted a point of slight weakness, because on the later standard engines which included much banking and propelling work in their duties, those of the 2-8-0, 2-6-0, and 2-6-2 tank type, two struts were provided from the base of the smokebox to the buffer beam. This feature was evidently not considered necessary on the express passenger locomotives. However, at least one of the 'Atlantics', No 187 *Bride of Lammermoor*, had plate struts fitted as shown in the photograph on page 44. A last point about the front-end was that No 98, like No 100, had lever reverse, although screw reverse had been usual on Great Western express locomotives for some time previously. This detail had an interesting sidelight on driving practice that will be discussed later.

One important feature of 4-6-0 design on the Great Western was not finalised on No 98. On his larger express passenger engines Dean had used Stroudley's arrangement of having the slide valves accommodated beneath the cylinders and driven by direct acting Stephenson's link motion. When it became necessary to change from 2-2-2 and 2-4-0 types to bogie engines, the presence of the valve chests immediately below the cylinders made it extremely awkward to provide the customary mounting for a bogie and Dean designed an adaptation of his centreless carriage bogie for his larger locomotives, in which all the weight was taken on side supports, and no more than a light framework was used to provide a guide for the bogie pivot, which took no weight. This could not have been adapted to an engine with large outside cylinders, and so Churchward turned again to American practice. In these the loads were applied to the axle boxes by equalising bars, and the bogie was connected to the engine frame by swing links. These latter proved troublesome, however, and experiments were made to obtain more satisfactory wear from their pivots. Concern was also expressed at the amount of flange wear that began to develop on the leading coupled wheels. While the swing links allowed freedom of lateral movement of the bogie, and consequently at the front of the engine, in so doing it caused the leading coupled flanges to do a considerable part of the work of guiding the engine into curves.

These, however, were teething troubles, and the general performance of engine No 98, very much better than that of No 100, gave promise of complete ultimate success. Despite this, however, the original 4-6-0 express engine remained a worthwhile traffic unit, and although in due course it was fitted with a standard taper boiler, and superheated, the original cylinders were never replaced. The castings permitted the valve chests to be bored out from the original 6½ in to 7½ in diameter, and with no more than this one change the front-end remained unaltered until the engine was taken out of traffic in 1932, and scrapped. It was, until then, working in the regular express link at Landore Shed, Swansea, and could be readily distinguished from the remaining engines of the class by the distinctive shape of its cylinders.

In 1903 the old style of painting for Great Western locomotives was still fully in vogue, for passenger, goods and shunting alike. As applied to the new 4-6-0s it was as ornate as in

4-6-0 No 2900 (originally No 100) on an up South Wales express near Reading, photographed not long before her withdrawal (the late M.W. Earley).

the most colourful days of Dean. The boiler barrel, firebox, cab and tender panels were painted in the familiar Brunswick green, which was retained to the very end of steam on the Western Region of British Railways, but the lining out was much more elaborate. Engine No 98 had four intermediate bands of colour on the boiler, one in line with the safety valve cover, one at the junction of the coned and parallel portions of the barrel, and two more between that and the smokebox. The tender sides were lined into three panels, and in the central one was the monogram with the scroll-letters GWR entwined. Everything below the running plate was in Tuscan red, including the wheel centres, under frames and footsteps. The side panels of the coupled wheel splashers were also painted red. More than one of the celebrated lithographed colour plates published by *The Railway Magazine* show the crossheads also painted red, though this is not confirmed in any of the 'F. Moore' paintings. The polished brass safety valve cover, and copper topped chimney completed a truly gorgeous turn-out which needless to say was immaculately kept.

Chapter 3

The French connection

From quite early broad gauge days on the Great Western, Daniel Gooch had a primitive kind of dynamometer car, modestly called a measuring van, which was used for a variety of purposes in addition to measuring the drawbar pull of locomotives. On the London and North Western Railway, F.W. Webb had a rather more sophisticated type of car, a six-wheeler, which was used for measuring the drawbar pull of locomotives, even down to such twentieth century types as the Whale 'Precursor' Class 4-4-0s. It was, however, through Churchward's interest in American practice that, even before he had succeeded Dean in the Chair at Swindon, authority was obtained to build a dynamometer car of modern design, in 1901. Characteristically for those days, little was heard about it at the time, and one of the earliest references to its existence, and then without any technical details, was in 1903, when Churchward lent it to Wilson Worsdell, of the North Eastern Railway, to test his then gigantic 'Atlantic' engine No 532, the first of the very impressive 'V' Class. *The Locomotive Magazine* recorded that on Saturday, November 21 it went north on the 2.20 pm Scotsman from Kings Cross, hauled by the pioneer large Ivatt 'Atlantic' of the GNR No 251, and that a record of that engine's performance was also taken on the journey north.

For Churchward the dynamometer car was invaluable. Although the records compiled were not anything approaching as comprehensive as those obtained in the same car after its modernisation in the late 1930s, by means of the separate measuring wheel it provided a continuous record of the speed throughout the trip, while the integrating apparatus gave a summation of the total work done. At that early stage in Great Western testing history a record of the coal consumption was made by direct measurement of the tender before and after a run. At that time, however, Churchward was far less concerned with the finer points of fuel consumption than with the drawbar records.

The improvements in boiler performance, valve gear, were to him all incidental to the job of getting a high sustained power output at high speed. He set himself a target of a drawbar pull of 2 tons at 70 mph and when engine No 98 gave him this figure he was satisfied, and refinements in design, and means of reducing coal consumption and maintenance costs could follow. In view of the initial embargo on the use of the new ten-wheeled engines in the London area, the tests on No 98 were carried out between Swindon and Weston-super-Mare.

Next, Churchward's interest in American locomotive affairs was once again shown when he obtained authority to build a stationary locomotive testing plant, the first in Europe, at Swindon. This was in the style of the one already in use at Purdue University and similar to that of the Pennsylvania Railroad currently being installed at the St Louis Exposition, and afterwards to be set up permanently at Altoona Works.

The Swindon plant was completed in 1904. Its primary purpose was to carry out tests on new locomotives under stable conditions, away from all the variations of traffic, weather and gradients that affected running out on the line. But Churchward was above all a realist, who appreciated that once his range of standard locomotives was fully established there would be little for such a plant to do, and little or nothing to justify the cost of maintaining machinery that represented a high capital investment. The additional use was thus envisaged of using the plant for running-in new, or newly repaired locomotives instead of taking them 'trial-trip', light engine, on the open road. The line, both east and west of Swindon, was at all times busily occupied with ordinary traffic, particularly in those days of many slow moving goods and mineral trains.

Churchward himself described its construction in a paper presented to the summer meeting of the Institution of Mechanical Engineers in 1904, in Chicago, of all places, thus: 'The Great Western Railway Co, have recently put down in their erecting shop at Swindon a plant for testing locomotives. This machine consists of a bed made of cast-iron, bolted on a concrete foundation, with timber baulks interposed for the lessening of vibration. On this bed five pairs of bearings are arranged to slide longitudinally so that they may be adjusted for any centres of wheels that are to be put upon the plant. In these bearings axles are carried having wheels fitted with steel tyres, on which the locomotive runs. These axles are also fitted with drums on which band-brakes act for absorbing wholly or in part the power developed by the engine. Outside these band-brakes, pulleys having an 18-inch face are provided at each end of the axle for driving link-belts, by which it is intended to transmit the major portion of the power developed by the engine to air-compressors, so that it may not be wasted.

'The hydraulic brakes will then only absorb just enough power to enable them to govern the speed of the engine. These brakes are actuated by a water-supply from an independent pump, the outlet of this water-supply being throttled either by a stop-valve or by a throttle actuated by a contrifugal governor. This latter device enables the speed of the engine to be set at any required number of revolutions and kept constant.

'The carrying wheels are 4 feet 1½ inches diameter. The main bearings are 14 inches long by 9 inches diameter. The tyre of the carrying wheels is turned to approximately the same section on the tread as the rails in use on the Great Western line. This plant is intended not only for the purpose of scientific experiment, but also for doing away with the trial trips of new and repaired engines on the main line. It has therefore been necessary to make it rapidly adjustable to take engines having wheels of different centres. The main bed is provided with a rack, and each pair of bearings is provided with a cross-shaft having a pinion at either end. These cross-shafts are driven from a longitudinal shaft through suitable clutches, and this longitudinal shaft is operated by electric motor and is capable of being reversed. The engine being run over the machine on an elevated frame which carries it on the flanges of its tyres clear of the carrying wheels, it is an easy matter to slide these carrying wheels with their bearings till they are vertically underneath the wheels of the engines to be tested. The frame is then lowered electrically and drops the engine into position on the carrying wheels.

'When running engines on trial trips, it is essential that the bogie and trailing wheels of engines so fitted should be run as well as the driving wheels, in order that the axle-boxes may take a good bearing, and be seen to be in a satisfactory condition before handing the engine over for traffic. To accomplish this, the carrying wheels are all coupled together by a suitable arrangement of belts and jockey pulleys. It therefore follows that, even when a locomotive having a single pair of driving wheels is run on the plant, all the carrying wheels are rotating and in turn run the bogie and trailing wheels of the locomotive. The jockey pulleys are necessary to retain the proper tension on the belts when the bearings are moved longitudinally.

'Owing to the varying height of the foot-plates of different classes of engine, it has been found necessary to provide a firing stage which can be rapidly adjusted vertically. A large coal bunk and weighing machines are provided in connection with this stage. Two water-tanks are mounted on the same plat-form, for measuring the water used when running, these tanks being emptied alternately when a consumption test is being made.

'Under the platform a dynamometer enables the drawbar-pull of the engine to be taken, and this, together with counters on the wheels, will enable the actual drawbar horse-power to be measured, and so compared with coal and water consumption for various classes of engines. As engines of different lengths are to be tested, and of necessity have to be fixed at the trailing end to the dynamo-meter, it is necessary to have a sliding chimney for carrying off the steam and smoke from the engine when running. This has been provided in the form of a long box, having a steel plate running on rollers forming its lower surface, which plate carries a large bell-mouthed chimney. This box not only enables the chimney to slide longitudinally, but will also form a receptacle for ashes and any other matter ejected by the engine, which will be retained and can be examined both for quantity and quality.

'It is hoped that this plant will enable many questions of the relative economy of different classes of engines, either simple or compound, to be settled definitely. The questions of super-heating and the efficiency of various forms of smoke-box arrangements might be investigated on it. The effect of various percentages of balancing can be investigated, and, in fact, any of the experiments which are at present being made on the road may be made on this plant, with the great advantage that any engine which may be selected can be placed in position ready for testing, and all connections made in a time probably not exceeding an hour.'

But for one reason or another the testing plant was little used, and it was not until many years later, when its equipment had

The first de Glehn 4-4-2 four-cylinder compound, purchased in 1903, No 102 La France *(British Railways).*

been modified, that it became the magnificent tool of engineering study and development invaluable in recent British locomotive history. On reflection, it is a little difficult to discern just what was in Churchward's mind in setting up the original plant, seeing that it was not capable of absorbing more than about 500 horsepower.

In the meantime, reverting to the year 1902, the 'French connection' with Swindon had begun before Churchward had been a year in the Chair. In its issue of January 3, 1903, *The Locomotive Magazine* was able to announce that construction of the de Glehn compound 'Atlantic' ordered from the Société Alsacienne, of Belfort was well in hand, though actually it was not until October 1903 that the engine was delivered at Swindon. In March of the following year, M Edouard Sauvage, Chief Consulting Engineer to the Western Railway of France, read a notable paper to the Institution of Mechanical Engineers, in London, entitled *Compound Locomotives in France.* It was a remarkable exposition covering no less than 54 pages of the institution's proceedings.

Mr Alfred de Glehn himself opened the subsequent discussion, but particular interest is attached to Mr Churchward's remarks. He is reported thus: 'There was no doubt in his own mind, and probably none also in those of the members present, that the compound locomotive had been developed to a point of greater perfection in France than in any other country in the world. It was his strong opinion to that effect which induced him to advise the Great Western Railway Directors to purchase one of those locomotives for experiment. A large number of so-called trials or tests between simple and compound locomotives had been made all over the world, but in his judgement no really fair and square tests between the advantages of compound and simple cylinder engines had ever been made. It would be found that some of the earliest tests between compound and simple locomotives which were made in this country were made between a compound engine, on the one hand, having 200 lbs, to the square inch in the boiler, and a simple engine having 175 lbs, per square inch. Quite naturally, the compound engine had the best of it, and that settled the point for the time. He was sorry to say that even in America that opinion still obtained to some extent, and in France also it had been the same. He would no doubt be told that the high pressures were used in the compound in the belief that it was impossible by any known valve-gear to use the same high pressures to advantage in a simple cylinder. He had thought that that had yet to be proved, and had had the courage to fit a simple engine with 18-inch by 30-inch cylinders, with a boiler carrying 225 lbs, to the square inch. He had done that with the deliberate idea of finding whether such improvements could be made in valve-gear, and consequent steam distribution, as to enable the simple cylinder to use steam of that pressure as efficiently as the compound engine.

'With the further view to make sure that the tests as between a simple and compound engine should be on quite equal terms, he had managed to arrange that the power—at any rate the powers at high speeds such as were now used for passenger trains—of the compound was practically identical with the power of the simple. It had been arranged that equal power should be given on the basis of a cut-off of the compound engine, as recommended by Mr de Glehn, of 55 and 65 in the high and low pressure respectively, and a cut-off of something between 20 and 25 per cent in the simple cylinders. It would seem no doubt ambitious to expect such power as was developed at 55 and 65 by the compound locomotive out of a cylinder in a simple engine cutting off at 20 to 25 per cent; but he was pleased to say that with the assistance of an efficient staff, a good deal of very hard work, and a determination to see what was possible to be done with the valve-gear, he believed such improvements had been made in the

steam distribution that a satisfactory result could be ensured from as high a cut-off as 15 to 20 per cent. In a test which had been made of the 18-inch by 30-inch stroke cylinders, of which he had been speaking, they had obtained, at 70 miles an hour, a draw-bar pull of 2 tons behind the tender. Upon a test which had recently been made with Mr de Glehn's engine, *La France*, that had also obtained a draw-bar pull of 2 tons at 70 miles an hour. The cut-off in the case of a compound engine was as advised, 55 and 65; and the cut-off in the simple engine was 25. The pressure used in the simple engine was only 200 lbs, to the square inch, so that in the simple engine carrying 225 lbs, to the square inch he thought it was legitimate to expect that the 2 tons at 75 miles an hour would be obtained with a rather higher cut-off than 25 per cent.

'The question which would immediately occur to all engineers was, what was the amount of steam used in the cylinders respectively on the two engines to give the pull of 2 tons at 70 miles an hour? The theoretical amount of steam in the 18-inch by 30-inch cylinder with 25 per cent cut-off was practically identical with that which there was in the high-pressure cylinders of the compound locomotive at the 55 cut-off; so that, if those figures were appreciated, engineers would no doubt understand that he had on foot, at any rate, means for a more equal trial between a compound and simple locomotive than had ever been made before. He would not like any one

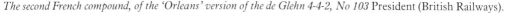

The second French compound, of the 'Orleans' version of the de Glehn 4-4-2, No 103 President (British Railways).

to take anything he was saying as to the results of trials between the French compound locomotive *La France* and engines on the Great Western as final or definite, because it would be obvious to any who had practical experience in the running of locomotives that for so short a space of time, and with so little mileage as they had been able to do with the engines, it was fruitless to give any definite opinion upon results. He was endeavouring in what he was saying to give no definite opinion as to the accomplished results.

'The first question that would occur to an engineer's mind would be the relative coal-consumption. When one knew the various factors which went to make up high and low coal-consumption, one realised that nothing short of a 12-months' average was of any use in comparing the coal-consumption of one engine with another, and he did not propose to give anything of the kind. He would like to take the opportunity, as both Mr de Glehn and M Sauvage were present, to say that *La France* had been doing very first-class work indeed on the Great Western Railway. She had given every satisfaction, and had entirely fulfilled his expectations; the work she had been doing on some of the fastest trains was really very fine, and he thought had not been equalled by any of what he might perhaps be permitted to term the old-fashioned simple engines. Those present who had studied the actual draw-bar records, which to his mind was the only record that was worth talking about in regard to a locomotive, knew that a steady pull on the back of the tender of 2 tons at 70 miles an hour on a 6-foot 6-inch wheel, took, if he might use a colloquialism, a great deal of getting, and when they had it, it took a good deal of keeping up. But it was fair to say that the Great Western had two or three engines running today that would do that, and *La France* was one of them.'

As first delivered, the French compound was painted black, and was subsequently lined out in something similar to the London and North Western style. Apart from quite superficial modifications to suit the British loading gauge, the Great Western engine *La France* was identical to those currently doing such excellent work on the Northern Railway of France. The principal dimensions were:

Cylinders—high pressure	$13\frac{3}{8}$ in dia
	$25\frac{3}{16}$ in stroke
—low pressure	$22\frac{1}{16}$ in dia
	$25\frac{3}{16}$ in stroke
Coupled wheel diameter	6 ft 8½ in

Total heating surface	2,325 sq ft
Grate area	29.5 sq ft
Boiler pressure	227 lb per sq in
Adhesion weight	34.5 tons
Total engine weight	65.0 tons

The third Great Western express passenger 4-6-0, No 171, was built for direct competitive running against *La France* and was given a boiler of the same dimensions as that of No 98 but carrying a pressure of 225 lb per sq in. It was very amusing to see that the apparently 'official' photograph of No 171 was not that of the new engine at all, but one of No 98 doctored up! The Swindon drawing office was to some extent quite adept in producing official pictures of individual engines, by the simple process of painting out the true numbers and names, but in the case of No 171, the rendering on the cabside plate of the '171' gives the game away, while the nameplate *Albion*, as painted in, is much longer than the actual plate was. Faked photographs apart, No 171 was completed at Swindon in December 1903, and was soon doing very good work.

The appearance and running of *La France* created intense interest. Rous-Marten was one of the invited guests on the inaugural trip, from Paddington to Swindon, and although it involved no hard work he was amused at 'the astonishing crowds that had assembled alike at Paddington and along the line to see the new locomotive, even the piles of milk-cans at the outer end of the down platform being converted into private boxes and dress circle for the occasion, and the scene altogether was a most curious one'. But when the engine was put on to the down Exeter 'non-stop', albeit with a light load of only 160 tons, some highly significant work was performed.

On the journey down there were two signal stops, and ten other checks, causing a loss of 20¾ min, in running, and yet the train arrived at Exeter 6¾ min, early. The net time for the run of 193¾ miles was 182½ min, an average of 63.8 mph. Two individual feats were worthy of special note in view of comparisons that would undoubtedly be made with Great Western 4-6-0 performance. The first was an acceleration on dead level track to a sustained 85 mph, and the second followed a dead stand for signals at Wellington, just at the foot of the steep Whiteball incline. Here speed was gradually worked up until, on a 1 in 80 gradient, 48 mph was attained before the tunnel was entered. The drawbar horsepower in the first case would have been about 650, equal to a pull of about 1.3 tons, and in the second, the equivalent dhp was about 1100.

Although Churchward told the Institution of Mechanical Engineers that *La France* had achieved his performance target of a drawbar pull of 2 tons at 70 mph, and one could gather by inference that both *Albion* and No 98 had done the same, it is remarkable that no actual records of such work remained among the comprehensive collection of dynamometer car rolls in the drawing office at Swindon in the 1950s.

When I was doing the research work for my book *Fifty Years of Western Express Running*, to be published in 1954 in celebration of the fiftieth anniversary of the Ocean Mail record run of May 9, 1904, I was privileged to examine all the dynamometer car records they had, and though I found many taken with 'City' Class 4-4-0s, 'Counties', 'Atlantics' and 4-6-0s of that same era, there was nothing relating to *La France*, or, for that matter, to either of the Orleans type 'Atlantics', which were imported in 1905.

From the likeness of *La France* to the almost identical de Glehn compound 'Atlantics' of the Northern Railway of France, some details of performance given in M Sauvage's paper could be taken as representative of what *La France* could do.

La France climbing the Whiteball bank and accelerating to 48 mph on a gradient of 1 in 80 would have given an actual pull on the drawbar of 2.65 tons, and the equivalent figure, relating the effort to level track would be 3.9 tons. At that time the legal maximum speed anywhere in France was 74.5 mph so that there was no French equivalent of *La France*'s maximum speed of 85 mph on level track, with a train of 160 tons. So far as Churchward's own locomotives were concerned, Rous-Marten logged one instance of a speed of 69 mph up a slight gradient of 1 in 750 with a load of 320 tons. This represented an equivalent drawbar pull of 2.5 tons—a substantial advance upon his target. *Albion* was apparently doing so well by comparison

that it was felt her being a 4-6-0 gave an advantage over the Frenchman, and so, in October 1904, she was altered to an 'Atlantic' though with no change in nominal tractive effort, 23,090 lb.

The French connection was, however, by no means ended. Sauvage in his paper to the 'Mechanicals' in March 1904, had given details of the eight de Glehn compound 'Atlantics' recently built for the Paris-Orleans Railway. These locomotives were then the most powerful running in France. The paper gave details of some trial runs made in November 1903, in which indicated horsepower up to 1600 had been recorded at 70 mph, and Churchward decided he must have two similar engines for trial on the Great Western. These arrived in June 1905. But while high power output was the primary consideration, and the division of the drive between two axles formed the starting point for the ever-famous four-cylinder 4-6-0 development, the various features of the French engines that were different from contemporary Swindon practice were very carefully studied, and none with greater interest than the bogie.

It has been explained earlier that in devising a bogie for the new six-coupled engines the results had not been entirely satisfactory, and the beautifully smooth riding of *La France* provided some food for thought in the Swindon drawing office.

When *La France* was first put to work on the Great Western Railway, the interest of Churchward and his men was concentrated upon all the factors contributing to power output. The drawbar pull was what mattered. But then other points began to intrude. The organisation of the locomotive department, as it was also on the majority of English railways in pre-grouping days, kept the Locomotive Running Inspectors closely in touch with the inside staff. They were the eyes and ears of the Drawing Office, and they were frequently called into consultation by Churchward himself.

Speed mph	Gradient 1 in	Indicated horsepower	Drawbar pull actual	Pull related to level
60.8	level	1098	1.9	1.9
47.8	200R	960	2.09	2.59
75.7	level	993	1.08	1.08
63.0	200R	1450	2.20	2.75
77.0	200F	1444	1.62	1.12
54.3	200R	1303	2.60	3.10

R = Rising gradient   F = Falling gradient

The fact that men marked for promotion were given spells of intermediate responsibility at the out-stations, in addition to time in Main Works or the Drawing Office, was an indication of the extent to which all aspects of locomotive design, maintenance and running were coordinated in Churchward's time, and the running inspectors as a body were relied upon to keep the chief informed as to how the locomotives were doing. Their opinions were carefully and sympathetically considered, and these men regularly and critically riding on *La France* reported that she was the sweetest riding engine that had yet run on Great Western metals. Part of this was immediately attributed to her having four cylinders with the drive divided between the two coupled axles; but these experienced observers began to realise that there was more to it than the arrangement of the machinery.

La France was working in the London-Plymouth link, with a very sharply curved stretch of line west of Newton Abbot, and it became noticeable that she entered the curves, and reacted to the frequent successions of reverse curves much more smoothly than the Great Western engines. Their observations were in due course transmitted to Churchward, and eventually he decided to give the French bogie a trial. It was of quite different design from that used on the first three Great Western express passenger 4-6-0s and continued on the ten-wheeled engines built in

1905, to be mentioned later. In the de Glehn design the weight of the engine was transmitted to the bogie through sliding flat surfaces. The lower surface was on the bogie frame and the weight was applied to the upper surface by hemispherical cups, which allowed angular movement of the bogie relative to the engine frame. The side bearers by which the weight was transmitted downwards can be seen in the photograph of *La France*.

Meanwhile, the bogie centre pin on the engine frame engaged a centre block on the bogie, but lateral movement of the block relative to the bogie frame could take place under the control of springs. Movement of the bogie relative to the engine frame applied a force through these springs which tended to lead the engine frame into a curve. It was noticed also that the action of these springs tended to reduce any tendency of the front end of the engine to oscillate. Churchward did not adopt the French bogie in its entirety, but retained the equalising bar arrangement of wheel springing. The blend of Swindon and French practice that resulted was extremely successful; it was not, however, until the year 1908 that it was adopted as standard in all large bogie engines, though all ten-wheeled engines built previously were in due course modified. On the four-cylinder engines built prior to 1908, with the outside cylinders roughly in line with the rear pair of bogie wheels, one could see whether the bogie had

One of the 1905 batch of 4-6-0s, No 175, before naming. Later Viscount Churchill *(P.J.T. Reed).*

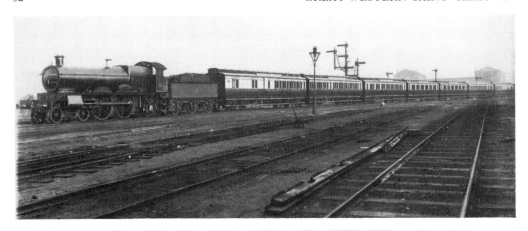

Top Albion, *as a 4-4-2, posed at Swindon, with the boat train built for the West Indian service, via Plymouth* (British Railways).

Above *The third French compound, No 103, photographed at Laira sheds, before naming* (P.J.T. Reed).

Below *One of the 1905 batch of 'Atlantics': No 182, later named* Lalla Rookh, *at Laira* (P.J.T. Reed).

been modified because the side bearers would be clearly visible. On the two-cylinder engines, they would be concealed behind the cylinders. There was more development to be done before this stage of finality in the design of these engines was to be reached.

To conclude this chapter there are two runs on the 10.50 am 2-hour non-stop express to Bristol on which the rivals can be contrasted, although the French compound had a much higher load. At the time the first run was made, *Albion* was relatively new and was under close observation with an inspector riding on the footplate. The sectional time-keeping was accurate, and after Didcot there was a comfortable margin in hand to offset the checks. The engine was driven hard from the foot of Dauntsey bank, because the maximum speed of 80 mph came some distance afterwards and speed was finely sustained up the subsequent rise to Corsham (Milepost 98). The French compound was not being driven very vigorously on this occasion, though the succession of checks must have been disheartening to the driver, Mr Dunn, whose very detailed log is the basis for the abbreviated version of the accompanying table, estimates that the check at Slough cost 3¼ min, and in consideration of the load of no more than 230 tons the subsequent running was not very enterprising.

GWR 10.50 am Paddington-Bristol

Date:				23-4-04		23-3-05	
Engine no:				171		102	
Engine name:				*Albion*		*La France*	
Type:				4-6-0		4-4-2	
Load (tons)—to Bath:				305		230	
—to Bristol:				275		200	

Distance miles		Schedule min	Actual m s	Speed mph	Actual m s	Speed mph
0.0	PADDINGTON	0	0 00	—	0 00	—
2.0	*Milepost 2*		4 08	—	4 17	—
5.0	*Milepost 5*		7 36	57	7 57	50
9.1	Southall	11	11 35	62	12 22	56
15.0	*Milepost 15*		17 11	65	18 18	63
—			—	—	pws	30
18.5	SLOUGH	20	20 17	70	22 24	—
21.0	*Milepost 21*		22 32	68	26 16	51
24.2	Maidenhead	25	25 32	64	29 49	56
31.0	Twyford		31 43	67/65	36 36	61
36.0	READING	36	36 15	68	41 29	65/55
40.0	*Milepost 40*		40 00	62	45 17	64
44.0	*Milepost 44*		43 50	63	49 01	64
48.0	*Milepost 48*		47 38	63	52 39	68
53.1	DIDCOT	53	52 18	64	57 05	68
56.0	*Milepost 56*		55 09	63	59 52	63
65.0	*Milepost 65*		63 58	62	68 42	60/62
69.0	*Milepost 69*		67 36	65	73 31	63
—			signals	—	signals	—
77.3	SWINDON	77	75 59	25	81 28	—
—			signals	—	signals	20
83.0	*Milepost 83*		83 38	62	89 28	62
88.0	*Milepost 88*		87 53	80	93 52	77
94.0	CHIPPENHAM	93	92 32	75	98 54	64
98.0	*Milepost 98*		95 56	70	102 52	58
—			pws	—	—	—
102.0	*Milepost 102*		100 42	65	106 35	78
—			—	—	signals	25
105.0	*Milepost 105*		103 21	70	110 53	—
106.9	BATH	107	105 14	25	113 08	—
114.0	*Milepost 114*		112 59	67	119 55	73
118.3	BRISTOL	120	118 09	—	125 03	—
	Net time (min)		113½		115	

Chapter 4

4-4-2 or 4-6-0?

The conversion of *Albion* from the 4-6-0 to the 4-4-2 type apparently made so little difference to her performance that for a time there seemed to be some doubt as to whether the standard main line passenger engine was to be a 4-6-0 after all. 'Atlantics' were being standardised on the Great Northern and North Eastern Railways, and it was not altogether a surprise when the *Locomotive Magazine* in its issue of January 1905 announced that three more 'Atlantics', identical to the modified *Albion* were in hand at Swindon, but that a further six 4-6-0s, similar to No 98, had also been authorised. In February the first of the new engines was out, and taking the next number from *Albion*, 172, it was named *Quicksilver*. It was the only 'Atlantic' to be built at that time, because the six anticipated 4-6-0s followed immediately. They took the next six running numbers 173-178, and their works' numbers showed that they followed consecutively from *Quicksilver*. This latter engine was Swindon Works' 2106 and the 4-6-0s that followed were 2107-2112. The fact that only one new 4-4-2 was built in the early months of 1905, against the three originally announced, might have seemed no more than incidental, since construction of 4-4-2s recommenced in April and 12 of them were built at Swindon between

then and September 1905, but No 172 gave them all a surprise, she would not steam!

When I was writing his biography, Sir William Stanier told me of the consternation this caused, to everyone from Churchward downwards. It was apparent the moment the engine had run her first trial trips, and it was probably this that led to the next two engines, Nos 173 and 174 being built as 4-6-0s, while the trouble with No 172 was sorted out.

The engine had apparently been stopped for examination in London. John Armstrong was then Divisional Locomotive, Carriage and Wagon Superintendent, but he was in America at the time, and Stanier, his assistant, was summoned to Swindon to meet an exceedingly irate Churchward, who wanted to know just what the hell was the matter with it. Stanier examined No 172 with great care, and said that the only difference from No 171 he could see was in the shape of the ashpan. When *Albion* had been converted to a 4-4-2 the original ashpan, carried down deep, and shaped round the rear coupled axle, had been left unaltered. Engine No 172 had a straight bottomed ashpan. On hearing this Churchward exclaimed: 'I think you've got it. We've restricted the air flow'. The engine was then altered to have a 4-6-0 ashpan and all was well. In the meantime Swindon built six new

Rivals in the trials of June 1905: the 4-4-2 No 172 Quicksilver, *with bowler-hatted officials on the footplate in addition to the engine crew* (P.J.T. Reed).

4-6-0s, before the resumption of 'Atlantic' building.

Only three of the new 4-6-0s were at first named, 173 *Robins Bolitho*, 174 *Barrymore* (soon afterwards extended to *Lord Barrymore*) and 178 *Kirkland*, named after a racehorse owned by one of the directors. At first the big engines did not normally work west of Bristol. One factor that could well have influenced the building of 12 more 'Atlantics' later in 1905 was the beautiful riding of the French compound *La France*, on the severely curved reaches of the South Devon line, and with *Albion* in her modified form showing equally good haulage ability between London and Bristol, it may well have been thought that the Swindon-built 'Atlantics' would give better riding than 4-6-0s west of Exeter. At that time Swindon had not produced its own version of the de Glehn bogie.

Churchward probably hesitated about reducing the adhesion weight, in view of the very severe gradients west of Newton Abbot, and in June 1905 comparative tests were carried out between Plymouth and Newton Abbot between the first of the new 4-4-2s, No 172 *Quicksilver*, with her altered ashpan, and the last of the new 4-6-0s, No 178 *Kirkland*. The trials were all made on the same day, with a train weighing 217 tons tare, including the dynamometer car, the test rolls from which I have had the privilege of studying.

Before discussing the interesting results of this one-day test in the west, which undoubtedly led to the regular use of 'Atlantics' on the Paddington-Plymouth run, three performances of *Albion* must be noted, all made at the time when use of the big engines was generally confined to the Paddington-Bristol section. On the first of the three, the dynamometer car was added to the ordinary load of the train, the 10.50 am from Paddington. The tare weight of the 13 coaches was no more than 337 tons, 26 tons apiece, but with the exception of the dynamometer car they were all of the Dean clerestory-roofed type, and they were pulling very heavily compared to more recent

There was gratification in the locomotive department when a drawbar pull of no less than 3 tons was registered between Uffington and Shrivenham, at 60 mph, on a rising gradient of 1 in 754, but this would indicate a coach resistance of something like 17 lb per ton, a very high figure by later standards, which were reckoned at about 11 or 12 per ton at 60 mph. In view of the resistance of the coaching stock his engines had to pull in the early 1900s, one can understand that Churchward's main concern was at first concentrated on getting high tractive power. In his collateral responsibility for carriage design one can be sure he was equally anxious to reduce coach resistance.

Charles Rous-Marten clocked two runs with *Albion* on the 10.50 am express from Paddington, one when the engine was in its original condition, as a 4-6-0, and one after its conversion to an 'Atlantic', but they gave results exactly opposite to what would have been expected. The load was 320 tons in each case, and the engine did much the better work uphill as an 'Atlantic' and the fastest downhill running when it was a 4-6-0. On the long gradual rise through the Vale of the White Horse, towards Swindon, the 'Atlantic' maintained a speed of 63 to 65 mph, whereas the 4-6-0 was doing 56 to 58 mph. Allowing for the lighter load, *Albion* as an 'Atlantic' must have been exerting a drawbar pull of at least 3 tons on that gradual ascent. The train was then scheduled non-stop from Paddington to Bristol, 118.4 miles in 2 hours, and making careful allowance for signal delays experienced, both engines would have kept time comfortably, though on the 4-6-0 trip the arrival in Bristol was 2 min late. The net times were 115 min (4-6-0) and 114 min (4-4-2). The maximum speed on the 4-6-0 trip was 80 mph.

The records of Rev W.A. Dunn, who lived at Bath for many years, include a very much finer performance of *Albion* in her original 4-6-0 days (April 23 1904 to be exact), when a load of 305 tons was taken from Paddington to Bristol in 118 min, 9 sec, or 113½ min net. Rev Dunn was a most meticulous recorder, and his log includes the time at practically every milepost en route. The train passed the 75th post in 73 min, 12 sec from the start, the average speed for 70 miles having been 64.1 mph. There was a bad signal check approaching Swindon, and another through the Box Tunnel, but Bath was passed in 105¼ min, at the usual much reduced speed, and Bristol reached 1½ min early. A notable feature of the run was the very steadily maintained speed once 60 mph had been attained. In the 67 miles between Posts 8 and 75 there was no greater variation than between 62 and 70 mph. This became characteristic of the rock-steady steaming conditions on Great Western locomotives.

Rous-Marten having arrived at an entirely negative result in his own investigations, one

The 4-6-0 rival, No 178 Kirkland, *at Laira* (P.J.T. Reed).

can turn with even greater interest to the one-day trial of 4-6-0 versus 4-4-2 on June 18, 1905, on the South Devon line. So far as drawbar pull was concerned, attention was concentrated on the climbing of the exceptional inclines, on each side of Dainton tunnel, from Totnes to Rattery signal box, and from Plympton up to Hemerdon Siding.

The accompanying gradient profile of the line between Newton Abbot and Plymouth will convey something of the overall task set to locomotives. When the Cornish Riviera Express was put on, in 1904, running non-stop between London and Plymouth, via Bristol, the time allowance for the 31.9 miles between Newton Abbot and Plymouth was 44½ min, although this involved an average speed of no more than 43 mph over this very difficult section, the curves are such as to preclude any maximum speeds of more than 60 mph anywhere between Newton Abbot and Hemerdon, and on the downhill sections the running was usually restrained to much less, quite apart from the prescribed restrictions at Newton Abbot itself, Totnes, Brent, and Ivybridge. It was only in the descent of the Hemerdon incline where the line is fairly straight that speed was allowed to rise to as much as 70 mph. On the day of the 4-6-0 *versus* 4-4-2 tests, the weather was fine, though the apparent sure-footedness of the 'Atlantic' on the exceptional gradients was such as to presage their regular use to Plymouth before the year 1905 was out.

The tabulated details herewith are taken from a close examination of the dynamometer car charts. On the westbound runs there was really nothing to choose between the two engines. *Quicksilver* made the faster time up Dainton bank, apparently because cut-off was

advanced from 32 to 40 per cent ¾ mile before the similar adjustment took place on *Kirkland*. On the Rattery incline, the 4-6-0 got a better 'run' at the bank through passing Totnes at 55½ mph, against 51½ mph, but, again, cut-off was advanced to 40 per cent earlier on the 'Atlantic', so that by Milepost 225 the 4-6-0 had fallen slightly behind on speed. But having topped the worst part of the bank, at Tigley box (Milepost 226), the 'Atlantic' was notched up to 32 per cent, whereas the 4-6-0 continued at 40 per cent to make better time over the upper and easier part of the bank.

Eastbound, on both climbs, the 'Atlantic' was at a disadvantage from lower initial speeds at both Plympton and Totnes, but the severe banks were nevertheless climbed with competence. On Hemerdon bank it will be seen that a cut-off of 51 per cent was used from Milepost 241. Both the 4-4-2 and the 4-6-0 had the notched lever type of reverser control, and while towards mid-gear this provided for a fairly fine adjustment of cut-off, above 32 per cent one notch meant a relative large increase in power.

The two additional 'Atlantics' forecast at the beginning of the year were completed at Swindon in May 1905, Nos 179 and 180. The first of them was named *Magnet*, the derivation of which I have not been able to determine. In June the two Orleans type compound 'Atlantics' arrived from de Glehn's works in Belfort, and took their places in the Paddington-Plymouth link, and then Swindon got to work in earnest, building ten more 'Atlantics', Nos 181-190 between July and October 1905. At first only one of them was named, No 184 *Churchill* after the Chairman of the GWR.

GWR dynamometer car test runs: 18-6-05

South Devon line—load: 217 tons

Engine type:	4-4-2		4-6-0	
Engine no:	172		178	
Engine name:	*Quicksilver*		*Kirkland*	
HEMERDON BANK	**Average speed milepost to milepost mph**	**Cut-off per cent**	**Average speed milepost to milepost mph**	**Cut-off per cent**
Milepost 242	—	32	—	27
Milepost 241½	45.0	40	52.9	32
Milepost 241	36.0	51	45.0	40
Milepost 240¾	30.0	51	37.5	40
Milepost 240½	26.5	51	32.1	40
Milepost 240¼	23.1	51	27.3	40
Milepost 240	20.4	51	24.3	51
Milepost 239¾	17.7	51	20.4	51
Milepost 239½	15.0	51	18.0	51
Milepost 239¼	20.4	51	23.7	32
Speed at Plympton (mph)	46		55	
Speed at Hemerdon (mph)	14½		18	
Total time Posts 242-239¼	6 min 32 sec		5 min 28 sec	
DAINTON BANK				
Milepost 223	—		—	
Milepost 222	31.5	27	39.2	27
Milepost 221	41.8	27	47.4	27
Milepost 220½	42.9	27	46.2	29
Milepost 220	45.0	29	46.2	29
Milepost 219	48.0	32	49.3	32
Milepost 218¾	43.0	32	45.0	32
Milepost 218½	40.9	32	40.9	32
Milepost 218¼	33.4	32	33.4	32
Milepost 218	25.7	32	26.5	32
Milepost 217¾	23.1	32	23.7	32
Speed at Totnes (mph)	26½		35½	
Speed at Post 220¼ (mph)	49		51	
Speed at Dainton (mph)	21		22½	
Total time Posts 223-218	8 min 21 sec		7 min 40 sec	

Another of the 1905 'Atlantics' No 181 Ivanhoe (P.J.T. Reed).

GWR Dynamometer car test runs: 18-6-05

South Devon line—load: 217 tons

Engine type:	4-4-2		4-6-0	
Engine no:	172		178	
Engine name:	*Quicksilver*		*Kirkland*	
DAINTON BANK	Average speed milepost to milepost mph	Cut-off per cent	Average speed milepost to milepost mph	Cut-off per cent
Milepost 215	—	32	—	32
Milepost 216	41.9	40	43.4	32
Milepost 216¼	45.0	40	45.0	32
Milepost 216½	43.0	40	43.0	32
Milepost 216¾	40.9	40	39.2	40
Milepost 217	39.2	40	36.0	40
Milepost 217¼	34.0	40	32.2	40
Milepost 217½	29.1	40	27.3	40
Milepost 217¾	24.3	40	21.4	40
Milepost 218	23.7	40	22.5	40
Maximum speed (mph)	46.5		46.5	
Minimum speed (mph)	22.5		19	
Total time Posts 215-218	4 min 54 sec		5 min 15 sec	
RATTERY BANK				
Milepost 223	—		—	
Milepost 223½	50.0	32	52.9	32
Milepost 224	45.0	32	48.7	32
Milepost 224¼	40.9	40	43.0	32
Milepost 224½	36.0	40	39.2	32
Milepost 224¾	33.3	40	34.6	32
Milepost 225	31.1	40	30.0	40
Milepost 225¼	29.1	40	28.1	40
Milepost 225½	27.3	40	26.4	40
Milepost 225¾	25.7	40	25.0	40
Milepost 226	28.1	32	29.1	40
Milepost 226¼	30.0	32	31.1	40
Milepost 226½	30.0	32	33.4	40
Milepost 226¾	32.2	32	36.0	40
Milepost 227	33.4	32	37.5	40
Milepost 227¼	32.2	32	36.0	40
Milepost 227½	33.4	32	36.0	40
Speed at Totnes (mph)	51½		55½	
Speed at Tigley box (mph)	25½		25	
Speed at Rattery box (mph)	36½		38	
Total time Posts 223-227½	8 min 0 sec		7 min 39 sec	

By the end of October, the 'Atlantics' heavily outnumbered the 4-6-0s, because, including the three French compounds, there were 17 of them, against only eight of the 4-6-0 type. Six of the last mentioned, namely 98, 173, and 175 to 178 are included in a notable montage of engine photographs taken at Laira sheds, Plymouth, together with six 'Atlantics'. Among the latter are the two Orleans type compounds 103 and 104, and then 171, 172, 180, and 184. At the time this montage was prepared, only Nos 171, 172, 173 and 178 were named, which dates the photographs concerned as prior to the late autumn of 1906.

An interesting comparison of the work of French and English 'Atlantics' when the Cornish Riviera Express was running via Bristol is provided in the accompanying tabulation. Both were hauling what was then the standard train set, weighing 197 tons tare. Both engines had London drivers of unsurpassed reputation at that time. The French compound, No 103, afterwards named *President* was driven by J. Springthorpe, who in later years took the engine *Polar Star* for its experimental running on the LNWR between Euston and Crewe. The Swindon 'Atlantic' No 180, afterwards *Coeur de Lion*, was driven by W. Butcher, the No 1 engineman at Old

Oak, among whose special assignments was the working of royal specials. Perhaps the most notable occasion was the funeral journey of the late King Edward VII from Paddington to Windsor, in May 1910, when among his passengers were no fewer than *nine* reigning monarchs. Churchward himself accompanied Driver Butcher on the footplate. It was said then that 'at no time in the previous history of railways had any one man with his hand on the regulator controlled to an equal degree the destinies of Europe'.

GWR The up limited

Load: 197 tons tare, 210 tons pull.

		103	180
Engine no (4-4-2):		de Glehn	GWR
Engine type:		compound	type
Distance	**Schedule**	**Time**	**Time**
miles	**min**	**m s**	**m s**
0.0 PLYMOUTH (North Rd)		0 00	0 00
2.9 *Milepost 243*		5 15	5 05
6.9 *Milepost 239*		12 10	11 20
18.9 *Milepost 227*		28 33	25 15
23.1 Totnes		33 05	29 42
27.9 *Milepost 218*		38 55	35 57
31.8 NEWTON ABBOT	44½	44 10	41 25
52.0 EXETER	70	69 17	66 10
71.9 *Whiteball Box*		91 25	88 35
82.8 TAUNTON	101	100 35	97 50
125.9 *Milepost 120*		140 40	137 35
126.9 *Pylle Hill Junction*	143	143 45	139 50
128.6 *Bristol East Depot*		146 45	143 30
138.7 BATH	158	158 40	155 35
151.6 Chippenham		172 50	169 40
168.3 SWINDON	189	189 25	185 30
192.5 Didcot	212	211 10	207 37
209.6 READING	229	226 27	223 03
221.6 *Milepost 24*		237 31	234 33
237.6 *Milepost 8*		253 17	250 21
245.6 PADDINGTON	265	262 40	260 05

Passing now to an occasion less fraught with national and international significance, it will be seen from the table that driving the 'Atlantic' engine No 180 he was already more than 3 min ahead of the Frenchman as early as Totnes; but after that the going was very even throughout to Paddington. The permanent speed restrictions were then very severe, being 10 mph through the Dawlish tunnels, 5 mph at Exeter, 10 mph round the curves of the Bristol avoiding line, and 15 mph at Bath. Intermediately the respective average speeds over the unhindered stretches of line were:

Engine no	103	180
Ascent to Whiteball Tunnel		
(Posts 193-174)	54.9	55.5
Descent of Wellington Bank		
(Posts 172-165)	76.3	74.1

Engine no	103	180
Somerset coast levels		
(Posts 165-120)	64.6	65.2
Old main line (Posts 99-8)	63.8	63.2

In addition to the photographic evidence of this fascinating period in Great Western locomotive history I am fortunate in having the train running records compiled over 50 years by A.V. Goodyear and some of his intimate friends. Rous-Marten, Rev W.J. Scott, the Rev W.A. Dunn and in later years Cecil J. Allen travelled on the Great Western from time to time, and have left us much valuable data in their writings, but Goodyear specialised in the Great Western, and extending back to the late Autumn of 1905 the mass of accurately compiled data contained in his log books constitutes an invaluable bank of information on the performance of all types of Great Western express locomotives.

As early as December 1905, Churchward was according him footplate passes, a privilege never granted to Rous-Marten, or to Lord Monkswell, for that matter. He was still very active with his stop-watch after the Second World War, and it was then that I met him, and enjoyed many years of interesting correspondence with him and his friends in the West Midlands. He was actively recording up to the Autumn of 1961, but even after that his last notebook is packed with running details compiled by friends, including cuttings from some of my own articles in *The Railway Magazine*. After his death, I was honoured that these immaculately compiled notebooks should be bequeathed to me. Unlike his famous contemporary recorder, C. Rous-Marten, whose manuscripts were once likened to the result of an inked fly having dashed across the paper, Goodyear's pages were of an almost copybook neatness and clarity, and they remained so to the very end when he was passing his 80th year.

Two runs on the 10.50 am 2-hour Bristol express are of great interest as showing some of the earliest work of the Churchward engines built in 1905, and also the running of trains including the new massive-looking elliptical-roofed 68 ft corridor coaches, nicknamed the 'Dreadnoughts', which represented Churchward's first attempt to reduce the rolling resistance of coaching stock, by a much improved design of axle-box. Although much longer and heavier vehicles in themselves, their weight in relation to the number of passengers carried was much less. Together with details of the runs with the two engines of 1905 vintage, is one with a new 4-6-0 engine of 1906, the '2904', made very soon after its completion at Swindon. None of these engines was named at the time the runs were made, but for the record, they subsequently became *Robertson*, *Coeur de Lion*, and *Lady Godiva*.

On the first run, engine No 177 had a load of six 'Dreadnoughts', and three Dean clerestories, one of which was slipped at Bath. Engine No 180, an 'Atlantic', had eight 'Dreadnoughts' and three Deans, while No 2904 had a train described by Goodyear as 11 eight-wheelers and one six-wheeler. Particular interest is attached to the details of the first of the three runs, because Goodyear was on the footplate, and recorded some valuable information as to how the engine was being driven. It was unusual also in that the engine at that time was carrying a boiler pressure of only 200 lb per sq in, instead of the usual 225. This first run was the most unhindered of the three. The 'Atlantic' by contrast not only had a much heavier load, but had three severe checks, while on the third run fog conditions persisted for the first 20 miles out of London.

With the 4-6-0 No 177 a very rapid start was made out of London, with a speed of 60 mph attained by Acton (4.3 miles). The cut-off was then 25 per cent and the regulator three-quarters full open. It remained thus until Maidenhead was passed, when cut-off was shortened to 18 per cent. This working had been rather harder than would have been expected with these engines, but was no doubt accounted for by the lower boiler pressure being used on this occasion. There were slight checks before Goring and again nearing Swindon, but this did not prevent the train being nearly 4 min early on passing Bath. A reduction of speed to 15 mph was then required through this station, and a smart acceleration was needed to attain a maximum afterwards of 68 mph at Keynsham.

The 'Atlantic' engine, No 180, got a bad start out of London, with a slack to 10 mph over Hanwell viaduct, then under repair, but excellent work was done with this heavy train up the long and gradual rise to Swindon with an average of 63 mph from Didcot, and some very fast running followed. The average speed between Dauntsey and Chippenham (6.3 miles) was 77.3 mph and this, together with the subsequent average of 75.2 on to Box (7.9 miles) would have entailed maximum speeds of over 80 mph both on Dauntsey Bank itself and descending through the Box Tunnel. The signal check at Box itself was a bad one costing at least 2 min, but the engine was driven hard after releasing its two-coach slip portion at Bath, and attained 75 mph on the

GWR 10.50 am Paddington-Bristol

Engine no:			177	180	2904
Engine type:			4-6-0	4-4-2	4-6-0
Load (tons)—to Bath:			290	370	315
—to Bristol:			263	312	263
Distance miles		**Schedule min**	**Actual m s**	**Actual m s**	**Actual m s**
0.0	PADDINGTON	0	0 00	0 00	0 00
1.3	Westbourne Park		2 48	3 28	3 00
—			—	pw 10 mph	signals twice
9.1	Southall	12	11 30	14 28	14 05
—			—	—	signals
18.5	Slough	21½	20 20	24 18	24 12
—			—	signals	signals
24.3	Maidenhead	27	25 27	30 29	30 38
36.0	READING	39	36 25	42 27	42 40
—			signals	—	—
53.1	Didcot	56	53 28	58 34	57 24
—			signals	—	—
77.3	SWINDON	80	77 23	81 38	78 40
94.0	Chippenham	96	92 15	95 29	93 00
—			—	signals	pw 15 mph
106.9	BATH (Slip coach)	108	104 18	108 43	107 10
—			signals	—	—
118.4	BRISTOL	120	118 09	121 36	119 00
	Net time (min)		114	116¼	111½

level at Keynsham, though not enough to secure an absolutely punctual arrival in Bristol.

The third run, with engine No 2904 when brand new, was a very enterprising and impressive performance, in that the train arrived at Bristol a minute early after checks estimated to cost 7½ min. Because of the fog, and a heavy check at Taplow, the first 31 miles, to Twyford, took 38¼ min, but by then a speed of 69 mph had been regained, and the next 49 miles, to the summit of the line at Milepost 80, were covered at an average speed of 68.7 mph. Despite the checks in the early stages, the train was 1¼ min, ahead of time on passing Swindon, and there was no need for any exceptional speed downhill at Dauntsey, or through Box Tunnel. On passing Box station (101.9 miles) the average speed from the start was 63.3 mph. But there was a long slowing for track repairs between there and Bath, though the two slip coaches were delivered slightly ahead of time.

The most significant part of this run, however, was the slightly uphill section between Didcot and Swindon, covered at an average speed of 68 mph. Goodyear does not specify the exact composition of the train on this occasion, only that the estimated gross trailing load was 315 tons. Assuming, however, that it was the then-usual mixture of new elliptical, and Dean clerestory stock, the tractive resistance at 68 mph can be taken, conservatively, at 15 lb per ton, and on a gradient of 1 in 754 this would a drawbar pull of about 2.7 tons— a substantial improvement on Churchward's target of 2 tons at 70 mph. The 'Atlantic' engine No 180, on the second run in the table, was exerting a drawbar pull of about 2.3 tons at 63 mph, again a very satisfactory performance.

In referring in some detail to the performance of engine No 2904, in the interesting comparison it makes to the work of the earlier engines 177 and 180 on the same duty, I have stepped out of strict chronological sequence, because it was no doubt the experience of the winter of 1905-6 that went some way towards the decision to adopt the 4-6-0 type as the future standard.

Rous-Marten discussed the alternatives at some length in his articles in *The Railway Magazine*, but almost entirely from the viewpoint of adhesion. Churchward was building the 'County' Class outside cylinder 4-4-0s at that time, and Rous-Marten argued that if nothing more than a four-coupled engine was

needed, why go to the extra expense of an 'Atlantic'. It would, however, have been difficult to put a boiler of the steaming capacity of the Churchward 'Atlantics' on a 4-4-0 chassis, and I feel sure that the riding quality of the big engines on the sharply curved sections of the South Devon line was an important consideration. It was not until later that the cross-breeding between the Swindon and the de Glehn type of bogie, referred to in the previous chapter, was brought to finality, and it is probable that the 'Atlantics' rode more smoothly on curves than the 4-6-0s. As the runs with *Albion* and No 180 clearly demonstrated they were capable of absolutely first class work as 4-4-2s, and apart from *Albion* herself, which was converted back to a 4-6-0 in 1907, the remaining 13 continued as 'Atlantics' until 1912. By that time five of them, Nos 181, 182, 185, 188 and 189 had, in 1910, been superheated, and a further two, Nos 186 and 190, were similarly modernised in 1911.

The ten-wheeled engines, whether 4-4-2 or 4-6-0, had taken over completely the working of the 12 noon 2-hour express from Bristol to Paddington, and although the loads generally were not heavy, they gave very consistent results. A striking analysis of performance on this train was published in *Engineering* compiled from complete details of no fewer than 83 runs. The following details have been extracted. The train ran via Badminton, a distance of 117.6 miles, requiring an overall average speed of 57.8 mph.

Number of runs observed	83
Number with overall average speed of 60 mph, or more	58
Heaviest load (tons tare)	278
Lightest load (tons tare)	144
Fastest run, including delays (mph)	64.1
Slowest run, including delays (mph)	51.5
Fastest run, excluding delays (mph)	67.3
Slowest run, excluding delays (mph)	57.8

On the fastest run, after a late start of 12 min from Bristol, the time to Paddington was 111 min, including *six* intermediate delays. None of these was severe in itself, but the aggregate loss was 6 min, leaving a net time of 105 min and an average speed of 67.3 mph.

By the summer of 1906 the unusual situation, for the Great Western, had developed of having most of the latest and largest express locomotives unnamed, for in addition to 11 of the 'Atlantics', and three of the 1905 4-6-0s there were the ten new 4-6-0s

4-6-0 No 175 at Plymouth (North Road) after being named Viscount Churchill. *This picture shows the 'short-cone' taper boiler, and the original short smokebox* (P.J.T. Reed).

of May-June 1906, Nos 2901-10. The subsequent choice of names for these engines poses some interesting questions. In addition to *Albion*, two of the 'Atlantics' were named when new, Nos 179 *Magnet*, and 184 *Churchill*, the latter after the chairman of the GWR, Viscount Churchill. But then came the decision to use once again the names of the ten 4-4-0s of Daniel Gooch's design built by Robert Stephenson & Co in 1855. With one exception these engines had names of characters in the 'Waverley Novels' of Sir Walter Scott, though in three cases omission of the prefix 'the' might have led to misconceptions, and caused *Pirate*, for example, to be classified, by implication at least, alongside such London, Chatham and Dover Railway engine names as *Brigand* and *Corsair*. The other two Gooch 4-4-0s with the missing prefix were *Abbot* and *Antiquary*.

The broad gauge locomotive stock of the Great Western was distinguished only by names, no engines, even the humblest goods and shunting classes, had numbers. In the official locomotive lists it is interesting to find classes designated by the first one in the register alphabetically, and these Gooch 4-4-0s were known officially as the 'Abbot' Class, although the engine concerned was the eighth

to be built. It was the same with the very famous Gooch 8 ft 4-2-2s, known for the same reason as the 'Alma' Class.

The first built of those Gooch 4-4-0s of 1855 was the *Lalla Rookh*, and this name was revived on the Churchward 4-4-2 of 1905, No 182, and carried throughout the existence of this latter engine when numbered 2982. Moreover, in official GWR publications, the Gooch 4-4-0s are consistently referred to as the 'Lalla Rookh' Class. One can well be intrigued when all the remaining engines of the class were named after Scott characters.

In these days of computerisation, microchips, and all the semi-technical jargon that goes with them it is difficult to imagine an age when the reading of poetry was considered as much a part of the education of gentlefolk as the mastery of Latin and Greek, and while George Stephenson was struggling with his early locomotives at Killingworth Colliery the gentle Irish poet Thomas Moore had found such favour among the nobility that the Marquis of Lansdowne suggested that he should take up residence in the vicinity of his Wiltshire estates so as to have ready access to the magnificent libraries at Bowood House. It was in a cottage in the hamlet of Sloperton that Moore wrote the immense romantic epic

Above *An official picture of No 185 when named* Winterstroke, *showing the beautiful works plate mounted between the steam chest front covers. The name was later transferred to 4-6-0 No 176 and No 185 became* Peveril of the Peak (British Railways).

Below *A right-hand side view of No 186* Robin Hood *showing the lever reversing gear in the full reverse position* (P.J.T. Reed).

An interesting picture of No 187 Bride of Lammermoor *showing an experimental modification to the front-end framing, with a stiffening rib added. This engine has the later standard long-cone boiler, and extended smokebox* (P.J.T. Reed).

poem of *Lalla Rookh*, first published in 1817, the story of an Indian princess of quite exceptional virtue and beauty.

If Moore had been held in the highest literary esteem beforehand he touched the very pinnacle of contemporary fame with *Lalla Rookh*, a distinction he came to share with Scott. But whereas in this present age some of the 'Waverley Novels' have been adapted to the screen, and even to television, the great epic of *Lalla Rookh*, for which eminent publishers were at one time outbidding each other to gain publication rights, is little, if at all remembered. It is perhaps not surprising that the name should have been taken for a broad gauge locomotive when in the 1840s the publisher Longmans referred to it as 'the cream of the copyrights'. What is surprising, however, is that after the broad gauge 4-4-0 had been withdrawn, in December 1872, the name should have been revived 34 years later on the Churchward 'Atlantic', No 182.

The only one of the original names which was not used again on the Churchward 'Atlantic' was *Antiquary*, which was perhaps too near to 'antique' to be appropriate! The names originally carried by engines 171, 172, 179 and 184 were removed. The name *Albion* went into 'cold storage' for a year; *Viscount Churchill* was transferred to the 4-6-0 No 175, but the names *Quicksilver* and *Magnet* were not used again. The class then became:

171	*The Pirate*	184	*Guy Mannering*
172	*The Abbot*	185	*Peveril of the Peak*
179	*Quentin Durward*	186	*Robin Hood*
180	*Coeur de Lion*	187	*Bride of Lammermoor*

181	*Ivanhoe*	188	*Rob Roy*
182	*Lalla Rookh*	189	*Talisman*
183	*Red Gauntlet*	190	*Waverley*

The names not taken from the old broad gauge 'Lalla Rookh' Class were those used on engines 179, 184, 185, 187 and 189. That on No 183, mis-spelt as on its broad gauge predecessor, was afterwards corrected to *Redgauntlet*. When No 171 was converted back to a 4-6-0 in 1907, the original name *Albion* was restored. To complete the story of the naming of the Churchward engines of 1905, the three that had hitherto not been named became 175 *Viscount Churchill*, 176 *Winterstoke* and 177 *Robertson*.

Reverting to *Lalla Rookh*, I sometimes wonder if perpetuation of the name of a lady so reputedly beautiful and virtuous, the English for which is 'tulip cheek', was not the inspiration for naming the next series of Swindon 4-6-0s after 'Ladies', though not all were so beautiful or so virtuous as her. The 2901-2910 series of 4-6-0s were named thus:

2901	*Lady Superior*	2906	*Lady of Lynn*
2902	*Lady of the Lake*	2907	*Lady Disdain*
2903	*Lady of Lyons*	2908	*Lady of Quality*
2904	*Lady Godiva*	2909	*Lady of Provence*
2905	*Lady Macbeth*	2910	*Lady of Shalott*

That they proved real 'ladies' of the locomotive world goes almost without saying, as later chapters of this book will show, combining Sir W.S. Gilbert's 'grace of an odalisk, on a divan', with the strength of a modern all-in female wrestler!

Chapter 5

The broadening scene

The new batch of 4-6-0 express locomotives, Nos 2901-10, was completed in good time for the opening of the Castle Cary to Cogload line, which was authorised for through passenger trains as from July 2, 1906. The inaugural express train by that route, permitting of a 3-hour timing between Paddington and Exeter, was worked by the brand new 4-6-0, No 2902, which later became *Lady of the Lake*.

The opening of this new route, and the diversion of the more important West of England expresses to it, meant that additional trains had to be put on to the Paddington-Bristol route to cater for traffic previously carried by West of England trains. In the summer service of 1906, the Great Western had 31 runs of 100 miles and over made non-stop, though some of these, such as the 10.30 am Paddington to Exeter, were made by slip coach from a train additionally included as a non-stop from Paddington to Plymouth. There were also some long non-stop runs on the old Birmingham route, via Oxford, including one between Ealing Broadway and Birmingham, (123.6 miles) in 133 min. There was also, surprisingly, a non-stop run over the 119½ miles from Bristol to Shrewsbury.

Even with the 2901-10 batch of 4-6-0s available, the GWR had no more than 17 'Atlantics' and 16 4-6-0s to handle the heavy summer traffic, and there were none of the big engines to spare for the long non-stop runs on the Birmingham route, or for the Worcester non-stops. At the time the last mentioned trains were worked by Wolverhampton men on a cyclic diagram that involved a direct run to Paddington via Birmingham and Banbury, returning via Worcester.

So far as the new engines of the 2901-10 series were concerned, later to become the 'Ladies', they were easily distinguished, beyond the number spotting range, from the abandonment of the red underframes, wheels and splashers. A less discernible difference at long range was the introduction of the long-cone, instead of the half-cone boiler barrel, extending the tapering to the full extent from the firebox to the smokebox. Although nominally the same as the preceeding ten-wheeled engines, the cylinder diameter of the 'Ladies' was $18\frac{1}{8}$ in, except for No 2901 which was at

first something of a 'special'. She was the first Great Western engine to be superheated, and in fact the very first British locomotive to be so equipped. Six months later in that same year, 1906, George Hughes built two 0-6-0 goods engines with Schmidt superheaters for the Lancashire and Yorkshire Railway, with all the recommended accessories.

The accompanying drawing shows the arrangement of the Schmidt superheater applied to engine No 2901 when new. There were 24 elements in three rows of eight, and the layout followed the standard form that had been developed by its distinguished Prussian designer. Although it came to be widely adopted, and particularly so from 1910 onwards on the London and North Western Railway, Churchward objected to it on two grounds, the first economic, and the second that of day to day maintenance. The Schmidt superheater was heavily protected by patents, not only that, but its general use required the inclusion in locomotive designs of other proprietary articles, such as the special form of piston valve, mechanical lubrication, and so on.

Now Churchward was the last man to allow himself to become beholden to other people's specialised designs, and his practical objections to some of the constructional features of the Schmidt superheater led him to inaugurate a development of his own. The performance of engine No 2901 convinced him that superheating would be an advantage to the economic working of locomotives, but in view of the tremendous advance in tractive power that his 4-6-0s represented over the previous 4-4-0s, and the mastery they displayed over current time table demands, there was no immediate hurry, and time could be taken in developing a suitable apparatus. He did not consider a high degree of superheat was necessary, but based his development upon a steam temperature that would be just sufficient to ensure the absence of condensation in the cylinders.

In view of the spectacular improvements in performance that were afterwards achieved on certain other railways by the introduction of a *high* degree of superheat, one is curious to know just how much improvement Churchward secured by his more modest approach.

Top *The 3.30 pm West of England express, non-stop to Exeter, hauled by 4-6-0 No 178* Kirkland *(British Railways).*

Above *4-6-0 No 2909 when new and unnamed; later to become* Lady of Provence. *The reversing gear is in the forward position, with the lever out of sight* (P.J.T. Reed).

No comparative figures before and after superheating were ever published for the 'Saints' or for the four-cylinder 'Star' Class. The only dynamometer records which still exist of trial runs with the latter class show considerably better work with a non-super-heater engine of the 'Knight' series than with a superheated 'Queen', though the latter was not doing work which was a representation of the best of which these engines were capable.

So far as the two-cylinder engines were concerned, the concensus of opinion among the footplate men, conveyed back to head-quarters by the locomotive running inspectors, was that they worked better when not linked up below about 22 per cent, cut-off, and with the regulator no more than partially open. Theirs was just another case where the theoretically correct method of driving, with a fully open regulator and the shortest possible cut-off, did not apply. This viewpoint was supported in the drawing office at Swindon, and on the engines which had lever reversing gear, as on all the new 'Atlantics' and 4-6-0s up to and including the 'Ladies', notches for shorter cut-offs than 22 per cent were not provided.

In view of the use of the Schmidt super-

The second engine to be named Winterstoke, *the 4-6-0 No 176. This photograph is interesting as showing the short-cone type of taper boiler, but with extended smokebox* (P.J.T. Reed).

heater on engine No 2901, it is interesting to compare the proportions with those of other large two-cylinder 4-6-0s which were so fitted in pre-grouping days.

As first built, the Great Western engine No 2901 had cylinders of $18\frac{3}{8}$ in diameter, and for a short time carried a reduced boiler pressure of 200 lb per sq in, while the big Great Central 4-6-0 had the pressure subsequently raised to 180.

It was in 1906 that Churchward read his paper 'Large Locomotive Boilers' to the Institution of Mechanical Engineers, and it was in the subsequent discussion that James Stirling, late of the South Eastern Railway, and younger brother of the legendary Patrick Stirling of the Great Northern, chided Churchward for spoiling the appearance of British locomotives. In his dry Scots style he said, they were not 'bonny'. At the meeting Churchward passed off the comment lightly enough, but it must have struck a responsive chord in him somewhere, because in the next batch of two-cylinder 4-6-0s the angular aspect of the high raised running plate was greatly

softened by curving the steps at both the forward and the cab end. This new batch was fitted with screw reverse, instead of the previous notched lever, and it permitted of a finer degree of adjustment in cut-off, without the previous restriction below 22 per cent. I have seen engines of these later batches linked up to 18 per cent cut-off and provide very smooth and efficient running.

There seemed to be a rather quaint conceit in the infallibility of their engines prevalent in the locomotive department of the Great Western Railway at that time, for having produced, in 1906, a series of 'Ladies', they next went still better with a class of 'Saints'! The 20 engines of this series were all completed at Swindon in 1907. The names allocated to them provide an interesting, and at times intriguing study. It was natural to find included the four national saints of the British Isles, and also the founders of some of the best known monastic orders.

Then there was an admixture of the great martyrs of history, like *Saint Catherine* and *Saint Sebastian*, with figures whose names

Railway	Engine class	Boiler pressure psi	Combined total sq ft	Superheater HS sq ft
Great Western	No 2901	200	2104	307
Caledonian	'Cardean'	180	2330	515.8
Great Central	'Sir Sam Fay'	160	2817	430
London & South Western	No 15	180	2186	308

have far more modern associations, like *Saint Bernard* and *Saint Dunstan*. Engine No 2919 was originally intended to be *Saint Cecilia* but eventually took the road as *Saint Cuthbert*, thus reducing still further the number of female saints included. *Saint Helena* will no doubt be more familiar as the isle of banishment for Napolean I, rather than as a result of the exploits of the lady herself, but I must admit to not having a clue as to who *Saint Agatha* was! 'Santa Claus' was not forgotten, on engine No 2926 *Saint Nicholas*, but a surprising omission was that of Saint Christopher, the patron saint of travellers. The complete list of the 'Saint' series of 20 engines was:

2911 *Saint Agatha*	2921 *Saint Dunstan*
2912 *Saint Ambrose*	2922 *Saint Gabriel*
2913 *Saint Andrew*	2923 *Saint George*
2914 *Saint Augustine*	2924 *Saint Helena*
2915 *Saint Bartholomew*	2925 *Saint Martin*
2916 *Saint Benedict*	2926 *Saint Nicholas*
2917 *Saint Bernard*	2927 *Saint Patrick*
2918 *Saint Catherine*	2928 *Saint Sebastian*
2919 *Saint Cuthbert*	2929 *Saint Stephen*
2920 *Saint David*	2930 *Saint Vincent*

By the year 1907, the two-cylinder 4-6-0s had some very important rivals, because following the success of the experimental four-cylinder 'Atlantic' No 40 *North Star* it was decided to build a series of similar engines, but of the 4-6-0 type, and the first ten of these, taking the names of some of the earliest broad gauge passenger engines, were also named after stars. They had the same boiler as the 2901-30 4-6-0s, but had cylinders of 14¼ in diameter by 26 in stroke. The nominal tractive effort was a little greater but the principal difference lay in the use of the Walschaerts valve gear. The division of the drive between the leading pair of coupled wheels made them smoother riding engines than the two-cylinder type, though in tractive ability there was little to choose between them.

In the years 1908-9 when only one or two examples were fitted experimentally with superheaters, A.V. Goodyear timed a number of runs with both classes on the West of England road, via Castle Cary, with results that will be discussed later, but at the moment the running of the crack expresses over the new route provides an extremely interesting exposition of the capacity of the two-cylinder 4-6-0s in their original non-superheated condition. Indeed, so fine was their work that in years prior to the major timetable decelerations of 1917 it was hard to distinguish between the best running of non-superheated and superheated units of the same class.

When the 3-hour Exeter expresses were put on, over the new route, the two-cylinder engines practically had the job to themselves. The two Orleans type de Glehn compounds took their share, but in 1907 the new four-cylinder 4-6-0 began to come upon the scene.

Engine No 2902 Lady of the Lake *as originally built, with long-cone taper boiler, short smokebox and the smaller diameter of chimney* (P.J.T. Reed).

But some superlative performances were turned in by 'Ladies' and the new 'Saints', and fortunately, from the recordings made by A.V. Goodyear and the Rev W.A. Dunn, and those collected from various sources by the late E.L. Bell, they are well documented. Details of six runs are tabulated, all of which conveyed slip portions to be detached at Westbury and Taunton.

In considering these runs in relation to more recent journeys, it must be recalled that the speed restriction for turn out on the 'Berks and Hants' line at Reading was then much more severe, and that with the trains passing through Westbury and Frome stations there were heavy slacks involved, which were afterwards eliminated by the construction of the by-pass lines in the 1930s. On the other hand, except at holiday times, loads were considerably lighter.

Another factor to be taken into account, however, was that relatively moderate speeds were at first run over the newly completed line between Castle Cary and Cogload Junction, reflected in the generous working time allowance of 24 min for 22.6 miles of what subsequently became regarded as real racing ground. Furthermore, the 'Berks and Hants' line itself, and the cut-off between Patney and Westbury were not originally constructed as high speed main lines, and they included curvature that compelled the maintenance of relatively moderate speed on the falling grades.

The first two runs in the table were made with loads that would be considered normal, except in the height of the holiday season. In 1907 a dynamometer car test run was made on the Cornish Riviera Express with the first of the four-cylinder simple engines to be built as a 4-6-0, No 4001 *Dog Star*, and leaving Paddington, the load, including the dynamometer car, was no more than 290 tons tare. Details of the running on the level between Paddington and Reading were subjected to an elaborate mathematical analysis by Professor W.E. Dalby, in his classic work *Steam Power*. Although this was something of a 'show' occasion, the acceleration from the start was considerably slower than with the two-cylinder engines, and while the speed had risen to 70 mph by Slough the time was 21 min 36 sec. This, it will be seen, was substantially bettered by the two-cylinder engines even when the holiday loads had risen to as much as 440 tons.

The *Saint Martin*, run No 2, made an exceptionally vigorous start, and ran substantially ahead of time all the way to Taunton. Especially notable on this run was the attainment of a maximum speed of 71½ mph on the generally rising gradients up the Kennet valley. Although a permanent-way check hindered the final stage of the climb to Savernake, the Westbury slip portion was detached nearly 5 min early. The maximum speeds quoted in the table against Westbury are the highest attained on the descent from

Engine No 2906 Lady of Lynn at Exeter, after fitting with the later standard large diameter chimney (P.J.T. Reed).

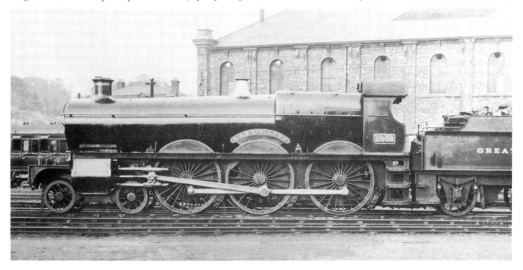

Engine No 2922 Saint Gabriel, *showing the modifications to framing on engines from No 2911 onwards, and screw reversing gear with the rod passing behind the nameplate, and permitting the fine works plate to be mounted on the splasher* (P.J.T. Reed).

Savernake, before speed was heavily reduced for the curves and junctions through Westbury itself.

Studying the times of runs 3, 4, 5 and 6 on the level start from Paddington to Reading, it will be appreciated that drivers were handling their engines to make a fairly rapid initial acceleration, with a speed of 60 mph attained soon after passing Ealing (5.7 miles), but not unduly pressing them to a high subsequent speed.

On the test run with the *Dog Star* the drawbar pull of the 290-ton train was 1.75 tons at 70 mph. From this one can deduce that on runs 3, 4, 5 and 6 the respective pulls were 2.0, 2.05, 2.55, and 2.60 tons, with corresponding drawbar horsepowers of 860, 885, 1045, and 1020. *Dog Star* was exerting no more than 730 on passing Slough, at 70 mph. It would seem that Professor Dalby was rather carried away by this latter fact, for he commented 'The author considers that the performance of the locomotive is remarkable. To exert a drawbar resistance of 1¾ tons at 70 mph corresponding to 730 horsepower at the drawbar, is an achievement in locomotive design which it would be difficult to surpass within the limits of the British loading gauge'.

The book from which I have quoted was published in 1915, but even in 1907 the performance was being substantially bettered by the 'Saint' Class engines in ordinary daily service. At that time, it is probably true that

such standards of working were confined to the Great Western Railway, but the performance of the 'Saint' Class engines, in their non-superheated condition, needs to be carefully born in mind for its subsequent relation to the work of the same engines when superheated.

The long upward pull from Reading to Savernake provides a severe test of sustained steaming capacity. From Milepost 38 (from Paddington) the line rises 415 ft in 32 miles, an average inclination of 1 in 410, but it is trying in that there is a severe concluding three miles from Bedwyn, where the gradient steepens to 1 in 190-141. On the four runs with loads of 340 tons, or more, the average speeds over this 32-mile stretch were 61.1, 57.1, 52.7 (checked) and 58.7 mph. On the third of these runs the net average speed was about 59 mph. On the three unchecked runs the equivalent drawbar horsepower works out at 1040, 973, and a remarkable 1210 for the engine *Lady of Lyons* on the sixth run in the table. The reduction of loads by the detaching of the slip portions lessened the demands upon locomotive power as the more severe gradients of the West Country were encountered, but the ascent of the Whiteball bank provides an interesting and significant test when the locomotive and its crew have been at work for more than 2½ hours, non-stop.

On the fifth run, with engine No 2923 *Saint George*, there were more passengers for the branch line destinations than could be accom-

GWR Paddington-Exeter

Run no:	1	2	3	4	5	6
Train ex-Paddington:	11.50 am	3.30pm	10.30am	3.30pm	3.30pm	3.30pm
Engine no:	2912	2925	2923	2923	2923	2903
Engine name:	Saint Ambrose	Saint Martin	Saint George	Saint George	Saint George	Lady of Lyons
Load (tons) —to Westbury	270	300	340	350	410	440
—to Taunton	235	265	307	300	350	360
—to Exeter	205	—	274	245	300	283

Distance miles		Schedule min	1 Actual m s	1 Speed mph	2 Actual m s	2 Speed mph	3 Actual m s	3 Speed mph	4 Actual m s	4 Speed mph	5 Actual m s	5 Speed mph	6 Actual m s	6 Speed mph
0.0	PADDINGTON	0	0 00	—	0 00	—	0 00	—	0 00	—	0 00	—	0 00	—
5.7	Ealing		8 21	—	7 37	—	8 22	58	9 15	—	8 35	—	8 47	56
9.1	Southall	11	11 47	65	10 48	70	12 19	63	12 48	—	12 00	68	12 13	60
18.5	Slough	20	20 39	—	19 19	—	20 30	72	21 15	72	20 39	—	20 43	65½
31.0	Twyford		32 22	—	30 33	71½	31 18	68	31 58	—	32 03	—	32 24	64½
36.0	READING	37	37 57	63½	35 00	—	35 51	20	36 38	—	36 46	check	37 20	—
53.1	Newbury	56	56 44	—	52 07	pw	54 55	63½	56 20	60	56 00	56	56 18	61
66.5	Bedwyn		70 18	—	64 03	—	67 40	62	70 04	—	72 38	check	69 33	60
70.1	Savernake	73½	74 21	46	69 01	—	72 03	53	74 10	51½	77 05	—	73 32	51½
95.6	WESTBURY	97½	96 52	74	92 42	77½	95 07	75	97 10	75	100 32	75	97 02	70½
101.3	Frome		103 41	51	99 37	51	103 26	—	104 28	—	—	—	103 38	—
108.5	Milepost 122¾	113½	—	77/45	—	74	112 42	51	113 15	49½	118 35	50	112 01	50
115.3	Castle Cary	120	117 43	—	113 54	74	119 50	74	119 35	—	124 35	—	118 43	—
137.9	Cogload Junction	144	140 11	—	138 57	—	141 39	—	141 50	—	145 21	—	142 20	—
142.9	TAUNTON	149	145 21	—	144 39	—	147 53	60	146 35	60	150 52	—	147 40	—
150.0	Wellington		153 20	—	—	—	—	53	153 48	56	9 31	54½	155 32	43
153.8	Whiteball	161	158 57	34	—	—	160 43	37	158 56	39	14 27	41¾	160 25	—
158.8	Tiverton Junction		163 57	76	—	—	—	75	163 44	—	18 59	—	166 00	—
173.7	EXETER	180	177 07	—	—	—	179 18	—	178 42	—	32 55	—	181 58	—

modated in the slip portions, and consequently stops had to be made at both Westbury and Taunton. From the latter, the climb of the Whiteball bank had to be made from a standing start, instead of an initial speed of about 60 mph.

The ascent of the Wellington bank begins in earnest at Milepost 166 (measured via Bristol) and continues for eight miles, details of these four climbs can be summarised thus:

Run no	3	4	5	6
Engine no	2923	2923	2923	2903
Load from Taunton (tons)	274	245	300	283
Time (min sec)	9 50	9 26	9 56	9 36
Average speed (mph)	48.8	50.9	48.3	50.0
Maximum speed (mph)	60	60	54.5	58
Minimum speed (mph)	37	39	41¾	43

The work of the engine No 2923 *Saint George* on No 5 run was outstanding seeing that it came from a standing start at Taunton, and that the minimum speed of 41¾ mph came at the entrance to the Whiteball Tunnel, on a gradient of 1 in 80, and that in the tunnel, where the grade eases to 1 in 127 there was a smart acceleration to 44 mph. It is very rare for speed to increase in the tunnel, and the acceleration in this case indicated an output of about 1150 equivalent drawbar horsepower. This was an exceptional figure at this speed. It may be added that on No 3 run, which was on the Cornish Riviera Express, running non-stop from Paddington to Plymouth, *Saint George* continued from Exeter, with a reduced load of 241 tons to cover the remaining 52 miles to Plymouth in 66½ min to arrive there just over a minute early.

In the eastbound direction Mr A.V. Goodyear made a special study of the working of the heavy 12.5 pm express from Exeter booked non-stop to Paddington via the new line in 3 hr 5 min. His very detailed analyses of the uphill running have made possible an interesting comparison of the results from the two-cylinder 'Saint' Class engines and the four-cylinder 'Stars', and not to the advantage of the latter. The collection includes a run with one of the first of the two-cylinder engines to be superheated, but also, notably, a fine performance by one of the 'Atlantics' sharing with the non-superheated 4-6-0 No 2912, the heaviest load of the series. Furthermore, although the 'Atlantic' was provided with a pilot from Exeter up to Whiteball summit she was left to tackle the steep ascent from Castle Cary to Milepost 122¾ unaided, and equally

the 18-mile ascent from Milepost 88 to Savernake. Both of these adverse sections were dealt with most competently, though it is true that the engine was favoured by fine weather. It might have been different on a wet day when the reduced adhesion of the 'Atlantic' could have been a handicap.

On the first of the six runs tabulated, *Saint Catherine* had a relatively light winter load, and was running comfortably ahead of booked time until the long succession of checks from Newbury inwards ruined the conclusion of the run. *Saint Gabriel* on the second run did almost as well uphill, despite a load 70 tons heavier, and the handicap of a strong wind. The minimum speed of 48½ mph at Whiteball summit was remarkable, but the descent to Taunton was taken at very moderate speed, and there were two slacks to 50 mph on the new line across to Castle Cary.

At about the same time Mr Goodyear clocked a run with the four-cylinder engine No 4009 *Shooting Star* on the same train, with an identical load, and the latter engine was consistently slower in climbing the banks and much faster downhill. This is not to suggest that the 'Saints' *could* not run fast, later chapters of this book effectively give the lie to any such idea, but the comparative uphill minimum speeds on these two runs are interesting: 48½ and 39 mph at Whiteball; 36 and 27¼ mph at Milepost 122¾. *Saint Gabriel* was almost stopped by signal in the approach to Westbury, but characteristically got very quickly into speed again to make one of the finest of all ascents to Savernake.

Before discussing the work eastwards from Westbury, which Mr Goodyear made the subject of a special analysis, the work on the remaining four runs up to this point requires some comment. *Lady of Quality* did relatively inferior work to Whiteball, losing 2¼ min on booked time, but ran hard down the Wellington bank, touching 78½ mph, and with a good climb to Milepost 122¾ was on time at that point. *Lady Macbeth*, by that time fitted with a standard Swindon superheater, although losing time up to Whiteball, ran much harder over the Cogload-Castle Cary section, which by that time had fully consolidated, and with a smart climb to Milepost 122¾ and a lowest speed of 36½ mph was there ahead of all other engines except the lightly loaded *Saint Catherine*. On the fifth run *Saint Ambrose* had a 14-coach train, which judging by its tare weight probably included a proportion of older stock, and would be pulling heavier than

Broadside view of No 2923 Saint George *showing position of the reversing screw in the cab* (P.J.T. Reed).

its actual tonnage would suggest. Be that as it may, after an initial loss of 3 min to Whiteball the crew did very well with their 420-ton load on a wet and windy day. A very severe slowing to 5 mph for bridge repairs put the train 4¾ min late on passing Castle Cary, despite which the climb to Milepost 122¾ was good, with a minimum speed of 33¼ mph. Nevertheless, Westbury was passed 5 minutes late.

The performance of the 'Atlantic' No 172 *The Abbot* requires special consideration. Although the train was made up to 13 vehicles, its tonnage was equal to the 14 of the previous run. Piloting of expresses up to Whiteball summit was a common occurrence at that time and all sorts and conditions of engines were used. Judging from contemporary photographs there always seemed to be any number of engines 'on shed' at Exeter, and the first thing available was put on. There is a record of *Lady Macbeth*, when relatively new, being turned out to assist a Dean 7 ft 8 in 4-2-2 which was working through from Newton Abbot to Bristol with a heavy train. The 'Atlantic' No 172 *The Abbot* had no less a celebrity than the *City of Truro* as pilot, and the two engines made a very fast ascent. The stop at the summit lasted 1 min 54 sec, and with a fast descent of the Wellington bank Cogload Junction was passed on time. Excellent work followed, and with a good climb to Milepost 122¾ (minimum speed 30¼ mph) Westbury was passed 1½ min early.

From Westbury to Savernake the schedule

time of 26 min for 25.5 miles was severe and no engine succeeded in observing it. The critical length is from Milepost 88 eastwards beginning with 6 miles continuously at 1 in 222. The minimum speed on the whole climb usually came at Milepost 82. The comparative performances of the two-cylinder and four-cylinder engines are most revealing from Mr Goodyear's records, thus:

Two-cylinder engines

Engine no	Name	Load tons	Time (Posts 88-70) m s	Minimum mph
2918	*Saint Catherine*	285	18 19	52
2926	*Saint Nicholas*	310	19 48	49
2922	*Saint Gabriel*	350	18 43	52
2908	*Lady of Quality*	375	20 00	46¾
2905	*Lady Macbeth★*	405	19 08	50
2912	*Saint Ambrose*	420	20 13	48

Four-cylinder engines

Engine no	Name	Load tons	Time (Posts 88-70) m s	Minimum mph
4021	*King Edward★*	305	19 55	—
4013	*Knight of St Patrick*	310	20 31	—
4013	*Knight of St Patrick*	310	17 03	—
4009	*Shooting Star*	350	19 23	—
4011	*Knight of the Garter*	350	19 28	—
4022	*King William*	350	21 05	—

★ Superheater engines

GWR 12.5 pm Exeter-Paddington

Distance miles		Schedule min	1	2	3	4	5	6
	Run no:		1	2	3	4	5	6
	Engine no:		2928	2922	2908	2905	2905	*172
	Engine name:		*Saint Catherine*	*Saint Gabriel*	*Lady of Quality*	*Lady Macbeth*	*Saint Ambrose*	*The Abbot*
	Load (coaches):		9	11	12	12	14	13
	Load (tons):		280	350	375	405	420	420
			Actual m s	**Actual** m s	**Actual** m s	**Actual** m s	**Actual** m s	**Actual** m s
0	EXETER	0	0 00	0 00	0 00	0 00	0 00	0 00
$7\frac{1}{4}$	Silverton		10 01	10 30	11 22	11 38	11 40	9 36
$14\frac{7}{8}$	Tiverton Junction		18 03	18 51	20 27	20 16	21 01	16 45
20	*Whiteball*	25	24 01	24 47	27 10	26 46	28 00	*22 00*
			—	—	—	—	—	pilot off
$30\frac{3}{4}$	TAUNTON	35	33 38	35 07	36 22	36 02	37 22	35 38
$35\frac{3}{4}$	*Cogload Junction*	40	38 25	40 18	40 45	40 26	41 43	39 52
			—	pws	—	—	pws	—
$58\frac{1}{4}$	Castle Cary	64	62 12	63 22	64 35	62 45	68 50	62 24
$65\frac{1}{8}$	*Milepost 122¾*	$73\frac{1}{2}$	70 46	71 47	73 29	71 06	77 57	71 31
$72\frac{1}{4}$	Frome		78 06	79 03	81 07	79 01	85 32	79 05
			—	signals	—	—	—	—
78	WESTBURY	$87\frac{1}{2}$	85 30	86 24	88 20	86 47	92 33	85 57
$85\frac{5}{8}$	*Milepost 88*		94 03	96 02	97 33	95 36	101 15	94 56
$91\frac{5}{8}$	*Milepost 82*		100 30	102 27	104 41	102 19	108 12	102 02
$103\frac{1}{2}$	Savernake	$113\frac{1}{2}$	112 22	114 45	117 33	114 44	121 28	115 46
$104\frac{5}{8}$	*Milepost 69*		113 21	115 55	118 45	115 55	122 44	116 53
$120\frac{5}{8}$	Newbury	130	Two stops	130 38	131 55	129 37	136 05	130 05
$134\frac{5}{8}$	*Milepost 39*		and three	144 32	143 41	141 44	147 59	141 45
$137\frac{5}{8}$	READING	148	checks	148 47	147 30	146 17	151 33	146 10
$139\frac{5}{8}$	*Milepost 34*			151 58	Four checks	149 29	154 24	148 51
				signals	and one stop	—	—	—
$155\frac{1}{4}$	Slough	166	172 52	166 48		164 16	169 03	163 48
$158\frac{5}{8}$	*Milepost 15*		176 47	169 48		167 21	172 08	167 01
			—	signals		—	—	—
$164\frac{1}{2}$	Southall	175	182 52	178 10		172 40	177 43	172 36
168	Ealing		186 17	181 33		175 43	180 47	pw 10
			—	—		signal stop	signal stop	signals
$173\frac{5}{8}$	PADDINGTON	185	193 31	188 55	194 52	186 05	190 56	187 50
	Net times (min)		183	$183\frac{1}{2}$	$184\frac{1}{2}$	183	185	$183\frac{1}{2}$
	Speeds Cullompton		59	58	$53\frac{1}{2}$	56	$51\frac{1}{2}$	$66\frac{1}{2}$
	Whiteball (mph)		41	$48\frac{1}{2}$	$36\frac{1}{2}$	$36\frac{1}{2}$	$34\frac{1}{2}$	—
	Milepost 122¾ (mph)		$38\frac{1}{2}$	36	31	33	$33\frac{1}{4}$	$30\frac{1}{4}$
	Savernake climb (mph)		52	52	$46\frac{1}{2}$	50	48	$48\frac{1}{2}$
	Maximum on run (mph)		$73\frac{1}{2}$	72	$78\frac{1}{2}$	79	$77\frac{1}{2}$	$78\frac{1}{2}$

*Pilot to Whiteball 4-4-0 No 3440 *City of Truro*

Summary of the two groups shows an average time of 19 min 22 sec for the two-cylinder engines with an average load of 358 tons, and 19 min 34 sec for the four-cylinder engines with an average load of 329 tons. This would suggest that on a bank of this nature the two-cylinder engines were one coach better than their four-cylinder counterparts.

The comparison would have been still more favourable to the four-cylinder engines had there not been included the exceptional run with the *Knight of St Patrick*, when Mr Goodyear was on the footplate and a special effort was being made for his benefit. The 'Atlantic' was doing well with the heavy 420-ton train, and the 6 miles of 1 in 222 ascent were covered at 61.5, 55.8, 52.9, 48.6, 45.6 and 43.9 mph. As will be seen from the main table, the train was well on time from Reading inwards until signal checks delayed the finish. Although it had a good start from so favourable a location as Whiteball summit, it was no mean achievement to pass Southall (144.7 miles from rest) in 148 min 42 sec, having regard to the uphill sections that had been negotiated, and the severe speed restrictions enforced at Frome, Westbury, and Reading. But the result might not have been so good on a wet day!

The final development of the Great main line network came in 1910 with the opening of the short route to Birmingham and the north, which enabled the company to run on equality of overall time with the London and North Western Railway between London and Birmingham. By that time Churchward had 40 of his 'Star' Class four-cylinder 4-6-0s at work, and a number of the two-cylinder 'Saints' could be released from West of England service to work on the new route.

At first the loads were not heavy. On the down 2-hour non-stop expresses coaches were slipped at Banbury and Leamington, and beyond the latter station the tonnage behind the tender was often little more than 200. In the up direction, slip portions of three, and some of the more notable runs in any detail, leaving relatively light loads for the 67.5 miles thence to Paddington. Before referring to some of the more not able runs in any detail, however, a pause must be made in this record of achievement on the road to the finishing touches in design represented by the addition of superheating and top feed apparatus. Before leaving the era of non-superheater engines there is a run of altogether outstanding quality to be noted. It was made on the 4.15 pm express from Paddington to Bristol, on May 15 1910, when that train was loaded to no less than nine, 70 ft coaches *plus* seven clerestory bogies, 485 tons tare and crowded with passengers just before the Whitsun holiday, at least 520 tons full. It was hauled by No 2930 *Saint Vincent*, then non-superheated. I must admit that the bare details of this extraordinary run would take some believing, had they not been recorded in complete detail by the Rev W.A. Dunn of Bath. He was then a regular traveller on the GWR and familiar with all the variations of loading, engine working and other details appertaining to the service.

The log of this most remarkable performance is shown in the accompanying table. The engine was worked extremely hard from the very start. Speed had reached 55 mph at Ealing Broadway, and the acceleration continued steadily until a maximum of 70 mph was attained, on level track, at Slough. This indicated a drawbar pull of no less than 3.1 tons, at this speed, thereby surpassing Churchward's basic target of 2 tons, aimed at in his original 4-6-0 development. This, it should be emphasised, was with a non-superheated locomotive, and at the time it was achieved it is safe to assert that no other British locomotive type had equalled, let alone surpassed such an achievement.

The engine must have been steaming freely, against the heavy demands made upon the boiler, because the effort was continued steadily up the gradually rising gradients towards Swindon, and at Milepost 70 after a rise averaging about 1 in 750 for 17 miles the speed was still 60 mph, and the drawbar pull about 3.4 tons. By then the train was getting several minutes ahead of time, and although there was a severe speed restriction to come after Wootton Bassett, the engine was eased a little. Passing Chippenham a little behind time there was a tremendous finish with a speed of 80 mph sustained for 3 miles between Box and Bathampton where the gradient is falling at 1 in 850. Mr Dunn's milepost timings show the speed to have been absolutely steady on this stretch, and a careful calculation suggests that the drawbar pull must have been around 3 tons—an outstanding feat at so high a speed. Details of this performance of 1910 must be borne in mind for comparison with some of the finest achievements of these engines after they had been fitted with superheaters. The driver was Croker, a Bristol man, but his fireman must also have displayed prodigies of energy and skill in providing the steam for such a superlative performance.

GWR 4.15 pm Paddington-Bath

Load: 16 coaches, 485 tons tare, 520 tons full.
Engine: No 2930 *Saint Vincent*.

Distance miles	Schedule min	Actual m s	Speed mph
0.0 PADDINGTON	0	0 00	—
2.0 *Milepost 2*		4 32	—
3.3 *Milepost 3¼*		6 12	46
5.0 *Milepost 5*		8 10	53
7.0 *Milepost 7*		10 19	57
9.1 Southall	12	12 58	60
11.0 *Milepost 11*		14 20	62
13.0 *Milepost 13*		16 10	65
16.0 *Milepost 16*		18 52	68
18.5 Slough	21	20 58	70
21.0 *Milepost 21*		23 13	68
24.2 Maidenhead	26½	25 56	67
36.0 READING	38	36 48	—
43.0 *Milepost 43*		43 00	—
53.1 Didcot	55	52 42	—
71.0 *Milepost 71*		70 32	60
77.3 SWINDON	80	77 50	45
—		pws	10
94.0 Chippenham	97	97 50	—
102.0 *Milepost 102*		105 15	79
104.0 *Milepost 104*		106 45	82
106.0 *Milepost 106*		108 18	64
106.9 BATH	111	111 13	—

Net time 105¼ min

Chapter 6

Finishing touches in design

Having produced locomotives that could put up the kind of performance described at the end of the preceeding chapter one might have imagined that Churchward would have been content, although such peak loading might have been thought to justify the development of the 'Pacific' design, beyond the solitary prototype of 1908, *The Great Bear*. But in those critical years of 1907-8-9 the staff at Swindon were being kept very busy in perfecting details of design which were, no doubt, to enhance the working efficiency of the basic 4-6-0s which had already been produced.

There is no question that the Running Department favoured the four-cylinder engines for long distance, high speed express work. Whether the enginemen themselves endorsed that opinion is not so certain. The four-cylinder engines were more comfortable to ride, of that there is no doubt, and in later years the work of the Bridge Stress Committee set up after the First World War showed also that they were much easier on the track. But up to the year 1913 Churchward himself seems to have had no very decided views, and after building the 'Queen' series of four-cylinder 4-6-0s in 1910, he reverted to the two-cylinder type in 1911.

By that time the design of the Swindon superheater had been finalised, and most of the intermediate development had taken place on 'Saint' Class engines. Reference has already been made to the fitting of the first of the 'Ladies', No 2901 *Lady Superior*, with a superheater of the Schmidt type. Then an apparatus of the American Cole type was tried on the four-cylinder engine No 4010 *Western Star*. This took place in 1907. Although including some detail features that were unduly complicated, it appealed to Churchward because the elements were straight and could be more easily removed. And it was this type of superheater that formed the basis of what became the standard Swindon pattern.

The first version of this latter was fitted to engine No 4011 *Knight of the Garter*, when this engine was built new, in March 1908. As in the case of the two-cylinder engine, No 2901 *Lady Superior*, it was the only one of the 'Knight' series originally fitted, and it was

perhaps a little strange that a comprehensive series of dynamometer car tests was made, not on No 4011, but on a later non-superheated member of the 'Knight' series, No 4013. But with the completion of engine No 4011 *Knight of the Garter*, Churchward had three superheater 4-6-0 engines running, and all round comparisons could be made.

The Swindon No 1 type, as the apparatus fitted to No 4011 was known, had three rows of elements, each having six units, and although the advantage of the Cole was in permitting the individual elements to be withdrawn through the smokebox, there were complications in the way the elements were made steamtight. Although it was immaterial, in that the same design of boiler was used on both classes, it was interesting in respect of the overall theme of this book that the later and final development of the Swindon superheater took place on engines of the 'Saint' Class.

The Swindon No 2 variety, like its predecessor, was fitted on only one engine, No 2922 *Saint Gabriel*, in October 1908. This also had three rows of elements each having six units. The tubes themselves were of smaller diameter than in the Swindon No 1, and the header bore much resemblance to the Cole type.

Then, in 1909, finality was attained in the No 3, in which there were only two rows, each containing seven units. The tubes were formed into units expanded into cast steel unit headers, which were fixed to the main header by stud fastenings, in an assembly that made removal of any group of elements a simple job, without disturbing any of the others. The No 3 superheater, which became the Swindon standard, was fitted to engine No 2913 *Saint Andrew*, and the design is shown in the accompanying drawing. This illustrates the original form with return boxes at the inner ends of the tubes. These were later superseded by 'U' return bends. The proportions of the five types of superheater used in the evolution of the standard No 3 are shown overleaf.

Early in my own engineering training I remember being made very much aware of the merits of the Swindon No 3 superheater, from the maintenance viewpoint, on a visit to Old Oak Common running sheds. A party of

Engine no	Date	Type	No of	Elements per row	Diameter of tubes	Heating surface sq ft
2901	1906	Schmidt	3	8	—	307
4010	1907	Cole	3	6	—	269
4011	1908	GW No1	3	6	$1\frac{3}{8}$ in	300
2922	1908	GW No2	3	6	$1\frac{1}{4}$ in	275
2913	1909	GW No3	2	7	1 in	262

Above *Mr Churchward off-duty!*

Below *The final development of the 'Saints': No 2934 'Butleigh Court', in photographic grey* (British Railways).

student and graduate members of the Institution of Mechanical Engineers was being shown round, and in the group to which I was attached was a man from the Northern Eastern Railway, so enthusiastic about his own company's practice as to be mildly critical of the Great Western. We came to a part of the yard where a 4-6-0, recently arrived after working one of the West of England expresses from Plymouth, had its smokebox door open prior to having the accumulated ash removed, and the subject switched to superheaters, with the North Eastern man criticising the relatively low degree of superheat used on Great Western engines.

At that time Sir Vincent Raven had turned from his initial use of the Schmidt superheater to the Robinson type, which was similar enough in its general style but sufficiently different to circumvent the German patents. Although originating on the Great Central, the Superheater Company had been formed to market the apparatus world wide, and by the early 1920s it was doing so very well. Its advertising slogan was 'A sound Running Shed Job'. Our Great Western guide at Old Oak that day went into the attack, and flatly disagreed that the 'Robinson' was a 'running shed job'. He argued that to give attention to the elements was a workshop job, requiring quite a lot of dismantling before any could be removed. Even a beginner like I was then could see how easy it was to remove elements from the Swindon type.

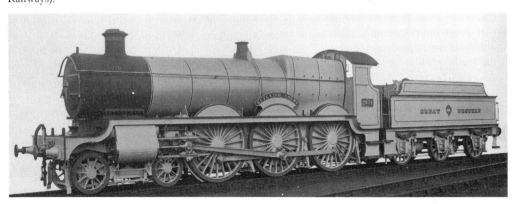

As to the degree of superheat used on Great Western engines, that will always be a point of controversy among locomotive men. Churchward did not favour a high degree of superheat, which would result in valuable heat being thrown away in the exhaust. He aimed at using the lowest degree of superheat that would ensure the absence of condensation in the cylinders. But to secure that ideal balance one had to be sure that the engine was steaming perfectly, otherwise a drop in boiler pressure would result in some condensation after the steam doing its work in the cylinders had expanded. With the moderate superheat attained in the standard Great Western 4-6-0s it would have been most interesting to have had a direct scientific comparison between the performance of superheated and non-superheated engines of the same class, relating coal and water consumption to indicated horsepower and drawbar pull.

That the 'Saints', in their non-superheated condition could do well-nigh phenomenal work is evident from the details of the run with the *Saint Vincent* discussed in the previous chapter, but the difference in driving methods from those used on the four-cylinder 'Stars' with Walschaerts valve gear may have contributed. The 'Saints' were usually run with longer cut-offs and a partly opened regulator and this latter condition, providing some wire-drawing, or throttling as it passed through the regulator valve, would tend to raise its temperature a little, and give a little superheat on its own account. It is a great pity, from the viewpoint of locomotive history, that a superheated and a non-superheated 'Saint' could not have been tested in 'all-out' conditions on the Swindon Stationary Test Plant. But of course at the time such a comparison could have been made, the plant itself could not have absorbed the power.

Deprived of any practical test results, one can indulge briefly in some theoretical considerations. First of all, superheating increases the volume of steam available for doing the job. Working at the Great Western pressure of 225 lb per sq in, the volume of 1 lb of steam in the non-superheated condition of 2 cu ft is increased to about 2¾ cu ft, if given the the moderate degree of superheat provided by the Swindon No 3 apparatus. If, by comparison, the results obtained with the Schmidt superheater on London and North Western engines are taken, using a boiler pressure of 175 lb per sq in, and steam superheated to about 650 deg F, against about 520 in Great Western engines, the volume of 1 lb of steam is increased to about 3½ cu ft. But if one equates the increased volume available to the reduced pressure the result is roughly a tie.

Churchward got his power by high boiler pressure, and avoided the lubrication problems that arose from the intensely dry searing action of highly superheated steam. According to Bowen Cooke's experience on the LNWR, the superheated tubes stood up to it well enough, it was in the piston valves and ports that carbonisation took place, and in due course affected engine performance. A further welcome factor arising from the use of superheating in any form was reduced water consumption.

Photographs taken of the 'Scott', 'Lady' and 'Saint' series of 4-6-0s when in their original condition show a chimney of slightly smaller diameter than that which subsequently became standard. It was a time when investigations were in progress to establish the ideal relationship between blast pipe tip, chimney height, and choke diameter. The outer shell of the chimney was actually made considerably larger than the true chimney inside, presumably so that experiments with the

Schmidt superheater on No 2901 Lady Superior (Institution of Mechanical Engineers).

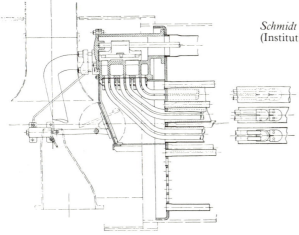

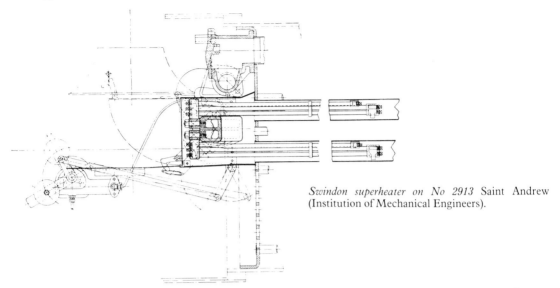

Swindon superheater on No 2913 Saint Andrew (Institution of Mechanical Engineers).

draughting could be made without affecting the outward appearance of the engine. We know that Churchward was quite sensitive to criticism of the appearance of his engines.

The standard design finalised on the No 1 boiler used on the 4-6-0s and the 2-8-0 is shown in the accompanying drawing and includes a choke diameter of 1 ft 3 in, and a diameter of 1 ft 7 in, at the chimney top. This drawing actually shows the cast-iron shaped chimney adopted as an economy measure during the First World War, to avoid the use of the ornate copper tops, but the inner chimney was always of the same proportions after finality had been attained, before 1910.

It was in that same year that another feature which became standard in Great Western practice was introduced, namely the jumper ring on the top of the blast pipe. This was intended to avoid the development of excessive back pressure when a locomotive was being worked hard. It consisted of a ring seating on the top of the blast pipe, from which a number of holes led into an annular space between the blast pipe top and the jumper ring. When the exhaust pressure rose above a certain predetermined value the jumper ring lifted, and when this occurred it increased the effective area of the blast pipe orifice by about 40 per cent.

Now the passage of exhaust steam through the blast pipe top at high speed creates the draught through the flue tubes for rapid combustion of the coal, and the harder an engine is worked, the more steam passes the blast pipe, creating a fiercer blast and an appropriately increased draught on the fire to promote more rapid combustion. But there comes a point when the fierceness of the blast increases to such an extent as to lift the smaller pieces of coal from the surface of the fire and throw them out of the chimney as red hot cinders. It was to check this effect that the jumper ring was introduced, for as soon as it lifted and increased the area of escape for the exhaust steam, the back pressure was reduced and the draught through the tubes greatly lessened.

The drawing of the Swindon No 3 superheater first fitted to engine No 2913 *Saint Andrew* shows the superheater header encased in a 'damper' box, which sealed off the outward end of the superheater from the smokebox. The doors of the damper were opened by small steam cylinders, when the regulator was opened, and closed when steam was shut off. When superheating was first introduced, it was thought it would be injurious to allow gases from the firebox to pass through the superheater flues when the tubes inside them were empty, and the dampers were to prevent any such gas flow.

On the Great Western the control of the damper doors was automatic, dependent upon the opening and closing of the regulator, but on the London and North Western, Bowen Cooke gave his drivers an independent control of the damper. This was sometimes used to great advantage when starting from 'cold' with a heavy train, when the fire was still a bit 'green'—to use the enginemen's term. Boiler pressure would be inclined to fall, and the

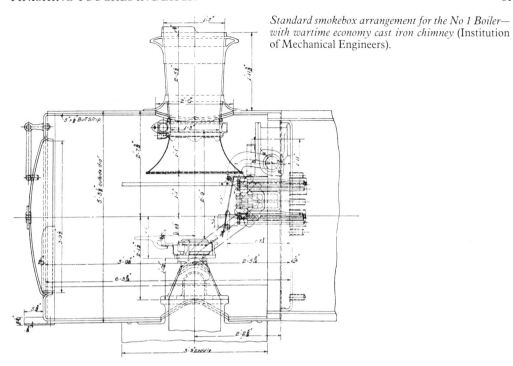

Standard smokebox arrangement for the No 1 Boiler— with wartime economy cast iron chimney (Institution of Mechanical Engineers).

Arrangement of top feed apparatus (Institution of Mechanical Engineers).

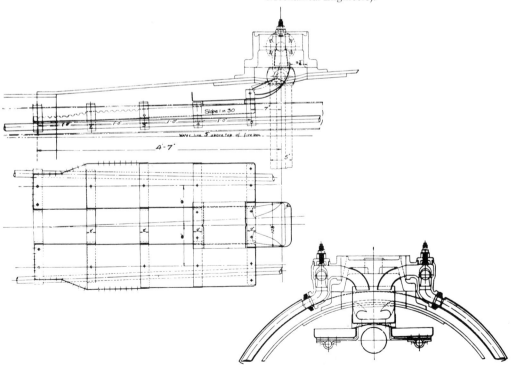

trick then was to close the dampers, and thus put all the exhaust gases through the small tubes. This quickly rallied the pressure, and the superheater dampers were opened again. Then they would get away to the vigorous starts characteristic of the Crewe superheater engines. It was not many years before superheater dampers were found generally unnecessary and they were discarded, not only on the Great Western and the LNWR, but elsewhere.

The introduction of superheating, and removal of the natural lubricating qualities of saturated steam, made it necessary to give special attention to cylinder lubrication, even though the conditions were less severe with the low degree of superheat used in Great Western engines compared to the far higher steam temperatures coming into use elsewhere. While his contemporaries were using various forms of mechanical lubricator, Churchward, characteristically, set out to perfect a design of his own that embodied a lubricator of the sight feed type, in which the driver could see the drops of oil passing through.

It was a beautifully contrived apparatus, the working of which could be observed when riding on the footplate. The principle was hydrostatic, with sight feed, controlled from the regulator handle. It had actually been introduced *before* superheating, but it was readily adaptable, and it supplied atomised oil into the steam pipes between the superheater header and the steam chest. Steam was fed from the steam fountain to a combining valve into which the oil entered from the lubricator. On the opening of the regulator, a quadrant was raised by a projecting pin which lifted the combining valve and allowed the steam to pick up the supply of oil, atomise it and deliver it to the steam pipes. But the arrangement also included a device that ensured a small amount of steam with oil was fed into the cylinders when running with the regulator closed.

This system of cylinder lubrication was a highly cherished feature of Great Western locomotives, so much so that in later years when higher degrees of superheat were introduced, and with them mechanical lubricators, the top link express enginemen always averred that the later engines were not so free-running as those which had the hydrostatic sight-feed lubricators.

After having built 40 engines of the four-cylinder 4-6-0 type Churchward reverted late in 1911 to the two-cylinder type for new construction, and they were the first of the 'Saint' Class to be built new with the standard Swindon superheater, and with the cylinder diameter increased to 18½ in. These engines included a new noticeable external feature in the top-feed clack valves fitted on each side of the safety valve bonnet. This was the result of another long and painstaking development at Swindon, under Churchward's direction.

That it was under consideration as early as 1906 was evident from the discussion on Churchward's paper to the institution of Mechanical Engineers, on 'Large Locomotive Boilers' when one speaker had suggested that the disadvantages of introducing a cold-water feed into the boiler could be mitigated by feeding the water into the steam space, well above the water line. It was a simpler way of doing it than using one of the proprietary forms of feed-water heater, which would of course, involve patent rights. Churchward assured the speaker that they were working on it, and intended to continue to do so until they had some positive results.

At that time boiler feed arrangement on the GWR varied. Some of the older engines, notably the Dean 7 ft 8 in single-wheelers, had an ornamental clack valve on the side of the boiler, while on Churchward's own earlier engines the feed was delivered at the bottom of the barrel, just behind the smokebox.

Although it was intended that the clack valves should be somewhere on the top of the boiler it was thought to be insufficient to dump the feed directly into the boiler. As with the lubricating oil feed to the cylinders it was thought that some degree of atomising was desirable, and the idea formed of allowing the feed water entering through the clack to pour downwards through a series of trays, through which it cascaded, getting hotter all the time, finally falling into the water in the form of a fine spray. The experiments to determine the shape and inclination of the trays were carried out on a 'hook-up' built in the open works yard at Swindon, on which a metered supply of water was fed over a series of trays. Early in 1911 the proportions of the device had been finalised, and the arrangement began to be fitted as standard to all Churchward's locomotives.

The first new design to appear incorporating the top-feed arrangement was that of the '43XX' mixed traffic 2-6-0, but the new series of two-cylinder 4-6-0s followed immediately afterwards. These were named after stately homes in the West Country, the first being No 2931 *Arlington Court*. One can, however, sense that the inspiration for the names of this particular series arose from Churchward's friendship with Neville Grenfell. Although an engineer to his fingertips, Churchward was very fond of country sports and was often a guest at Grenfell's home, Butleigh Court, not far from the 'cut-off' line from Castle Cary to Cogload, at Stoke Mandeville. It is perhaps significant that the official photograph of the 'Court' series of engines, in 'photographic grey' was not that of the pioneer, but of No 2934 *Butleigh Court*!

The new engines, of which there were 25 in all, were built in three batches, the first ten being completed at the end of 1911, and the second in the summer of 1912. The names and numbers of these 20 engines were:

2931 *Arlington Court*	2941 *Easton Court*
2932 *Ashton Court*	2942 *Fawley Court*
2933 *Bibury Court*	2943 *Hampton Court*
2934 *Butleigh Court*	2944 *Highnam Court*
2935 *Caynham Court*	2945 *Hillingdon Court*
2936 *Cefntilla Court*	2946 *Langford Court*
2937 *Clevedon Court*	2947 *Madresfield Court*
2938 *Corsham Court*	2948 *Stackpole Court*
2939 *Croome Court*	2949 *Stanford Court*
2904 *Dorney Court*	2950 *Taplow Court*

While the above included names that are well known in the West Country, perhaps the best known of all, that used on engine No 2943 did not refer to the well-known and famous royal residence at all, but to the relatively obscure Hampton Court, the very beautiful seat of the Arkwright family near Leominster, Hereford-shire. It is interesting that several of the names came from great family homes in the Welsh Border Country, such as *Caynham Court*, near Ludlow, and *Madresfield Court* near Malvern. But as with the 'Castle' Class engines in more recent times, no attempt seems to have been made to link the actual duties of the engines with their names, and as will be told later, *Hampton Court* came to distinguish itself greatly in a run on the 'Cornish Riviera Express'.

I have seen it suggested that the final order for 'Court' Class engines, to be built in 1913, was for ten, but that the last five were cancelled and replaced by five new 'Stars'. Be that as it may, the erecting shop at Swindon was switched without intermission from one type to the other, and No 4041 followed 2955 immediately. The last five 'Courts' were: 2951, *Tawstock Court*; 2952, *Twineham Court*; 2953, *Titley Court*; 2954, *Tockenham Court* and 2955, *Tortworth Court*. Engine No 2955 was evidently considered to be a unit of such significance as to be finished in photographic grey and posed for an official portrait, and it was this engine that represented the 'Saint' Class in the first of the list of Great Western locomoties issued officially from Paddington, in 1919. In the 4th edition of the enlarged publication, issued in 1946, the class was represented by No 2929 *Saint Helena*, which had been modernised at the front end with outside steam pipes.

Reverting to the year 1912, however, that year was significant in that it saw the conversion of the Churchward 'Atlantic' engines to the 4-6-0 type. Engine No 171, which was built as a 4-6-0 and temporarily

A record-making engine of 1912: 4-6-0 No 2943 Hampton Court *(P.J.T. Reed).*

altered, had been changed back again in 1907, all the rest were converted at various times during 1912, the last to be treated being No 180 *Coeur de Lion*. At the beginning of 1913, the engines built prior to 1906 were renumbered, bringing them uniformly into the 'Saint', or '2900' series. Engine Nos 171-190, became 2971 to 2990, while the two pioneers 100, and 98, became 2900 and 2998. Unlike some renumbering schemes on other railways which one can only recall with a sense of frustration, the new Great Western numbers were allocated in such a way that the originals could easily be identified.

By the summer of 1913, the two-cylinder series of 4-6-0s had thus been brought into a uniform group, and all eventually superheated. The numbering ran thus: 2900, originally No 100; 2901-10, 'Ladies'; 2911-30, 'Saints'; 2931-55, 'Courts'; 2971, originally No 171 *Albion*; 2971-90, Scotts etc and 2998 originally No 98. After the rebuildings of 1912 the only 'Atlantics' remaining on the GWR were the three French compounds Nos 102, 103 and 104, which were not renumbered.

The 'Saint', or '29XX' Class, as finally constituted, thus consisted of 77 engines. They were all uniform in their equipment, except that those built prior to 1907 had lever, instead of screw reversing gear; but more importantly No 2900 retained the original piston valves and valve gear with which it was equipped when first built in 1902, though the valves were subsequently enlarged to 7½ in from the original 6½ in. Valve setting, with the piston valves of 10 in diameter, was always treated as a matter of prime importance at Swindon.

On some railways using locomotives with the Stephenson link motion it was the practice to set the valves with equal lead at both ends of the piston stroke and allow the cut-off position to look after itself, but while this did provide a degree of smoothness in working

due to the equal cushioning effect on the pistons of the 'lead' steam, it did often result in an unequal amount of work being done by opposite ends of the cylinders, easily detectable by the varying loudness of the beat. Great Western locomotives had their valves set for equal cut-off and equal exhaust, and an actual valve card taken from engine No 2911 *Saint Agatha* in July 1907 shows the result of such setting. I have shown below only the details when the engine was in forward gear.

From the technicalities involved in these finishing touches to the truly great locomotive design, one can turn to the aesthetic and evocative appeal of these engines. Whatever James Stirling may have thought of them, a Great Western 'Saint' in pristine condition was a great sight. It was on the 2911-30 series, the 'Saints' themselves, that the heights of decorative elegance were attained, because in addition to the wealth of polished brass and copper work, the very splendid oval works plate was added on the splasher just below the nameplate. The polished brass beading on the splashers did not come at first, and it disappeared as an economy measure, in the Second World War. The long reversing rod, whether from lever or screw, was polished as lovingly as the connecting and coupling rods. The unusually broad sweeping round of the rods, due to the 30 in stroke, made these engines a tremendously impressive sight when starting away, and as a boy living at Reading in the early 1930s I had plenty of opportunity of seeing them thus.

I shall always remember one occasion, probably in 1911 when I had travelled from Mortimer into Reading with my Mother. We had just alighted when a down express drew in and stopped at the adjoining platform. The engine was the *Saint Benedict*, and the sight of those huge exposed driving wheels, brightly polished rods, and above all the height of the footplate above our platform level was almost overpowering.

Number of notch	Travel of valve	Steam cut-off		Exhaust opens		Exhaust closes	
		FS	BS	FS	BS	FS	BS
75%	6.25	22.85	22.66	28.16	28.1	28.16	28.1
70%		20.98	21				
60%		18.04	18				
50%		15.04	15.14				
40%		11.98	12				
30%		8.98	9.02				
25%	3.85	7.36	7.48	21.36	21.4	21.36	21.4
15%		4.26	4.44				

All dimensions in inches.
FS = forward stroke.
BS = back stroke.

Chapter 7

Varied and versatile performance

The introduction of the improved expresss service between Paddington and Birmingham in 1910, on the newly completed short route, via Bicester, opened up a new field of activity for the 'Saint' Class locomotives. One cannot say, however, that it was very demanding at first. It was a venturesome thing to challenge the long-established superiority in overall time held by the London and North Western, and the comfort and punctuality of the Euston trains combined with the innate courtesy of the service were qualities that Paddington would have to match.

Regular travellers do not readily change their habits, and on the Birmingham route one would be dealing essentially with a business rather than a holiday-going clientele. At the same time those regular travellers who were also railway enthusiasts quickly sampled the new trains, and details published in 1911 by Cecil J. Allen, in *The Railway Magazine* told their own tale, so far as train loadings were concerned.

When the new line was first opened for express traffic some of the constructional works on the purely new section between Ashendon Junction and Aynho Junction had not fully consolidated, and no more than moderate speed was run, over what later became a very fast stretch. The overall time of most of the express trains was 5 min over the even 2 hours.

On the few trains that were worked by Old Oak engines and men the three French compounds were sometimes used, but otherwise the 'Saints' had the service almost entirely to themselves during the first few years. A batch of them was allocated to Stafford Road shed, Wolverhampton, with drivers in a link that had established a reputation for outstandingly good work, hitherto with much smaller engines. This new allocation of 'Saint' Class locomotives followed

in the general tradition of the Great Western running department, in that the majority of London-bound expresses, whether from Bristol, South Wales, Worcester, or the West of England, were run by engines and men from the 'country' end. It was no more than natural that with express services from London operated to so many and so widely separated destinations, only a few top link Old Oak engines could be spared for each route. The men themselves knew all of them.

Reverting now to Allen's first experiences on this route, by the 9.10 am departure from Paddington, this was actually a 2-hour train, having one intermediate stop at High Wycombe, and detaching slip portions at Princes Risborough, and Leamington. The loads on his five runs were as shown below, in tons gross behind the tender.

All journeys were subject to a few out-of-course slacks, and no time could be booked against any engine; but it will be appreciated that with such light loads the demands for sustained power output were not very great.

One of the hardest trains on the new service was the 2.45 pm up from Brimingham, which carried a fair load through to London, but also a three-coach section that was slipped at Banbury and provided a through service from the north to Oxford and Reading. In consideration of its load, this train was at first allowed an extra 5 min overall. The working of this train became the subject of a very exhaustive analysis by Mr. A.V. Goodyear, but in quite early days it witnessed an engine performance that to my knowledge stands quite alone in the history of the 'Saint' Class locomotives. I should add that the 'Saints' allocated to Stafford Road shed at first were all in their original non-superheated condition.

It was only the second of Allen's runs over the route, and he was justifiably surprised to find a load of no less than 410 tons, from

Run no	1	2	3	4	5
Engine 4-6-0 no	2915	2912	178	2916	2924
Engine name	*Saint Bartholomew*	*Saint Ambrose*	*Kirkland*	*Saint Benedict*	*Saint Helena*
Load (tons)					
—to Princes Risborough:	270	280	260	240	200
—to Leamington:	245	255	235	215	175
—to Birmingham:	180	180	180	180	140
Total time (min)	122¼	120	120½	119½	121¾

Down West of England express passing Southall, hauled by an unidentified 'Saint', either of the 'Scott' or 'Lady' series.

Birmingham, to be reduced to 320 tons when the Banbury slip portion was detached. Although they started well from Leamington with this heavy train, some time had been lost through permanent way slacks on the new line and it took 66¾ min to pass High Wycombe, 60.8 miles. In addition to this, the train had been some 16 min late leaving Leamington, and while there was need for haste on a stretch of line favourably graded and well aligned for fast running, there is still astonishment in my mind as to what actually happened.

Allen described the event thus: 'Down the subsequent incline, after a positively uncanny rate of acceleration, we near the foot attained the phenomenal speed of exactly 90 miles per hour. I have not the least doubt in my own mind as to this maximum. I was able with my stop-watch to secure the record of ¼ mile in exactly 10 seconds for three alternative quarters—representing a total distance of 1¼ miles—so that this terrific rate was maintained for quite an appreciable distance—until we reached Ruislip troughs, to be exact. I was

in the last vehicle of the train, after the Banbury slip, and found the motion like that of sliding over a sheet of ice. The 17¼ miles from Beaconsfield to Park Royal were covered in 13 min 25 sec—average 77.1 miles per hour —and the 13 miles from Gerrards Cross in the extraordinary time of 9 min 45 sec—average exactly 80 miles per hour.'

The average speeds quoted need corrections, because in working them out he had apparently used the distances given in Bradshaw, which are only to the nearest quarter mile. Using the distances from the official working timetable the averages work out at 76.5 and 78.8 mph. This rather critical examination of this early record arises from the result being so generally out of keeping with the normal optimum performance of the 'Saint' Class locomotives as to arouse one's curiosity.

Out of the mass of data relative to the working of these engines on all parts of the Great Western Railway where they ran there are no more than a few instances in which they topped 80 mph. From my own records,

Engine no	2915	4049	5010	4049	4043
Engine name	Saint Bartholomew	Princess Maud	Restormel Castle	Princess Maud	Prince Henry
Average speeds (mph)					
Gerrards Cross to Ruislip	81.3	79.5	79.5	80.8	80.8
Gerrards Cross to Park Royal	78.8	77.6	78.8	78.3	77.3
Beaconsfield to Park Royal	76.5	73.8	73.3	75.3	73.3
Maximum speed (mph)	90	83½	84	83¾	85½

and from those of Mr Goodyear, I have looked out details of some fast descents of the Gerrards Cross bank, all with four-cylinder engines, and have set them alongside the feat claimed for the *Saint Bartholomew*, and while the average speeds over the fastest stretch, between Gerrards Cross and Ruislip, are all around 80 mph, the maximum speeds logged on the other four runs do not in any case exceed 85½ mph. This all goes to show that the crew of the *Saint Bartholomew* were making an exceptional effort on that occasion, because those engines, with the Stephenson link motion, did not readily and easily soar to such heights as their four-cylinder counterparts so frequently did.

Exciting as high maximum speeds may be to the recorder, and perhaps a little too exciting sometimes when riding on the footplate, it is the ability to accelerate rapidly and maintain a relatively high speed uphill that are the prime necessities for locomotives engaged in heavy main line express work, and these qualities the 'Saint' Class locomotives possessed in full measure.

After the short route to Birmingham was opened, A.V. Goodyear and his friends, between them, made so comprehensive a study of the running as to provide a positive 'bank' of information on the working of these engines. Details are now set out in the accompanying table of six runs on the mid-afternoon express from Birmingham to Paddington. Five of these were made after the train had been accelerated to a 2-hour run, inclusive of a stop at Leamington. The sixth,

with the heaviest load of all, was made on the original 125 min timing, but of such quality as to be fully up to the standard of running required by the quicker timing. The seventh was made on the same train but on an occasion when no Banbury slip portion was carried. Goodyear and his friends paid far greater attention to the uphill performance. They timed to specific mileposts in most cases, rather than to the centre of the adjoining stations, and the table can be considered in every way a specialist study.

The mileposts quoted in the table need some explanation; 92 is measured on the original broad gauge route to Birmingham, via Oxford; 14 is measured on the new line of 1910, from zero at Ashendon Junction; while 29 and 22 are measured from a zero at Northolt Junction points, ¼ mile on the London side of the station. The gradients on which the hill climbing performances are analysed are 1 in 187, up to Southam Road; 1 in 250 past Fenny Compton to Milepost 92; 1 in 200 from Aynho Junction up to Milepost 14; and Princes Risborough bank, beginning at 1 in 176-200, and then 2½ miles at 1 in 167 to Milepost 22.

The work of the superheater engine *Clevedon Court* on this particular bank was remarkable, with its minimum speed of 57¼ mph. This engine also produced the equally excellent speed of 61 mph at Milepost 14, after four miles at 1 in 200. These were no downhill speeds to compare with the meteoric flight of the *Saint Bartholomew* recorded by Cecil J. Allen. No actual maximum speeds are

Engine No 2905 Lady Macbeth *in wartime plain green.*

quoted in Goodyear's compilations, but from the milepost timings it would appear that engine No 2901 *Lady Superior* made the fastest descent, yet not greatly exceeding 80 mph. The Wolverhampton drivers who were responsible for these runs seemed to specialise in fast uphill work, making anything exceptional downhill unncessary. This makes the record Allen secured all the more extraordinary.

There is no mention as to whether engine No 2901 still retained the Schmidt superheater at the time of the run tabulated. As it was made in August 1912 it is probable that by then it had been replaced by a standard Swindon No 3 type. Schedule times were 26 min from Birmingham to Leamington, and 91 min thence to Paddington, and when allowance is made for the checks experienced there was no time to be booked against any of the seven engines.

On the down road details are tabulated of five runs on the non-stop 11.5 am express from Paddington, which slipped one or two coaches at Leamington. Although the loads at that period in the history of the line were lighter than those conveyed on a train like the 2.50 pm up from Snow Hill, the shape of the gradient profile was such that speeds were more nearly sustained on at least two of the major inclines, and a reasonably accurate estimate of the power output could be made. On the up journey, although the amount of hill climbing involved was, in the aggregate, the same, the worst inclines were on more varying gradients, and they could be rushed from a high initial speed.

On the up journey it was rare for speed to be held at a steady sustained figure on the 1 in 200 from Aynho Junction at Milepost 14 (near Ardley) and still less on the Princes Risborough bank. Going north, however, speeds were often well sustained between Gerrards Cross and Beaconsfield. After the speed restriction at High Wycombe, recovery had to be made against the stiff gradient up to Saunderton (Milepost 22¾), and the Bicester bank, 5½ miles at 1 in 200, often resulting in a sustained minimum near the top. In the accompanying table, in addition to five runs with 'Saint' Class engines there is also, in column 3, one with one of the larger French compound 'Atlantics'. A supplementary table has been prepared to show the performance on the three principal inclines.

Comparison of the actual running times with those booked from point to point suggest that the initial allowance of 30 min to passing High Wycombe was unduly tight, and it was only on the fourth run, with *Saint Benedict*, that anything near time was made. But there was margin for recovery over the new part of the line, and all six engines passed Aynho Junction on time. That *Saint Sebastian* (run No 2) managed to do this after two fairly severe checks was due to some quite exceptional running over the Ashendon-Aynho section with a minimum speed of no less than 62 mph at Ardley summit (Milepost 13) and, as shown in the table analysing power outputs, with the highest value of equivalent drawbar horsepower in the whole collection, 1218. This was the result of a drawbar pull of about 3 tons, at 62 mph. On the West Wycombe bank the best outputs resulted from drawbar pulls of around 3½ to 3¾ tons at 50 mph.

Turning now to the Paddington-Bristol route, it is of interest to recall that prior to the wartime alterations in timetabling, the 1.5 pm non-stop 2-hour express from Paddington carried no slip portions and ran via Badminton. Mr Goodyear's collection includes an excellent run made in May 1914 with engine No 2911 *Saint Agatha*, with a heavy train of 11 coaches, 360 tons with passengers and luggage. There was a bad check at Old Oak Common, so much so that the time to passing Southall was 14½ min, in some contrast to the vigorous starts made on the West of England trains and referred to in Chapter 5. But the engine ran well from Slough onwards and the 53 miles thence to Shrivenham were covered in 50½ min, against the gradually rising nature of the line. Despite the initial check, which had cost about 2 min, Milepost 76 was passed in 78 min 49 sec, but signals checked the approach to Swindon, and speed was eased a little over the junction at Wootton Bassett.

Once on to the Badminton line, however, some quite remarkable work was done. On the first favourable stretch down to Little Somerford, speed did not exceed 68 mph, but then the entire 10 miles of ascent to Badminton station, at 1 in 300, was climbed at an average speed of 62.8 mph, and over the last 5 miles the speed was steadily maintained at 60 mph, involving an output of 1190 equivalent drawbar horsepower. No very high speed was attempted down the long succeeding descent at 1 in 300; 72½ mph was sustained for seven miles continuously, and in passing Winterbourne (110 miles) in 111¾ min from Paddington there remained 8¼ min for the

GWR 2.50 pm Birmingham-Paddington

Run no:		1	2	3	4	5	6	7
Engine no:		2911	2926	2949	2909	2937	2901	2903
Engine name:		*Saint Agatha*	*Saint Nicholas*	*Stanford Court*	*Lady of Provence*	*Clevedon Court*	*Lady Superior*	*Lady of Lyons*
Load (tons gross)								
—to Banbury:		295	335	385	390	395	415	320
—to Paddington:		215	240	300	305	300	325	320
Distance		**Time**	**Time**	**Time**	**Time**	**Time**	**Time**	**Time**
miles		**m s**	**m s**	**m s**	**m s**	**m s**	**m s**	**m s**
0.0	Snow Hill	0 00	0 00	0 00	0 00	0 00	0 00	0 00
—		signals	—	signals	—	—	—	—
$3\frac{1}{4}$	Tyseley	5 35	5 12	5 45	5 26	5 32	5 30	5 20
7	Solihull	10 10	9 05	10 08	9 38	9 47	10 00	9 30
$17\frac{1}{8}$	Hatton Junction	20 35	17 32	20 00	19 33	19 13	19 40	23 08*
$21\frac{1}{4}$	Warwick	signals	signals	signals	23 25	22 45	23 03	26 32
$23\frac{1}{4}$	LEAMINGTON	checked	26 03	28 40	25 48	25 05	25 26	28 57
6	Southam Road	10 30	9 27	10 05	10 30	10 32	10 18	9 17
11	Fenny Compton	16 13	14 40	pw slack	16 05	16 11	16 03	14 35
14	*Milepost 92*	19 34	17 43	20 43	19 25	19 27	19 31	17 46
$19\frac{7}{8}$	BANBURY (SLIP)	24 35	22 35	26 00	24 40	24 30	25 00	22 57
$24\frac{3}{4}$	*Aynho Junction*	28 40	26 55	30 30	29 08	28 49	29 02	27 34
29	*Milepost 14*	32 26	31 03	34 48	33 37	32 54	33 17	31 51
34	Bicester	36 30	35 12	38 48	37 50	36 38	37 24	35 53
43	*Ashendon Junction*	44 17	43 08	46 55	45 05	44 01	45 15	44 01
$48\frac{1}{4}$	*Milepost 29*	49 46	47 39	52 06	50 41	48 41	50 18	48 50
$55\frac{1}{4}$	*Milepost 22*	56 42	54 53	59 26	57 52	55 19	58 26	56 27
$60\frac{3}{4}$	HIGH WYCOMBE	61 30	60 42	65 10	63 40	60 55	64 00	62 35
$65\frac{5}{8}$	Beaconsfield	67 20	66 25	70 40	69 12	66 55	69 05	68 28
77	Northolt Junction	77 28	76 47	80 32	78 52	77 23	78 28	78 13
$82\frac{3}{4}$	Park Royal	82 20	81 48	85 30	83 40	82 23	83 15	82 52
—		signals	—	signals	signals	—	signals	—
84	*Old Oak West Junction*	84 42	83 37	87 30	85 45	84 14	85 20	85 00
—		signals	—	signals	signals	—	signal stops	signals
$87\frac{3}{8}$	PADDINGTON	91 50	88 36	93 45	92 30	89 46	96 25	91 50
Net time Leamington-Paddington (min)		$89\frac{1}{2}$	$88\frac{1}{2}$	$90\frac{1}{2}$	$90\frac{1}{4}$	$89\frac{3}{4}$	90	90
Minimum speeds (mph)								
Southam Road		$41\frac{1}{4}$	$46\frac{3}{4}$	45	$44\frac{1}{2}$	$41\frac{1}{2}$	$41\frac{1}{4}$	$48\frac{1}{2}$
Milepost 92		$56\frac{3}{4}$	61	$53\frac{1}{2}$	55	56	$50\frac{1}{2}$	58
Milepost 14		58	56	$56\frac{1}{2}$	$53\frac{1}{2}$	61	57	56
Climbing of Princes Risborough bank Mileposts 29-22								
Average speed (mph)		60.5	58	57.2	58.1	63.2	51.6	55.3
Minimum speed (mph)		57	55	$51\frac{1}{2}$	$53\frac{1}{2}$	$57\frac{1}{2}$	$47\frac{1}{2}$	45

*Signal check

last seven and a half miles. With clear signals throughout it might have just been managed but there were many signal checks and the arrival was 4½ min late.

In the reverse direction the running of the 'Saint' Class engines on the non-stop 2-hour trains seemed to suggest that any load up to about 400 tons made not the slightest difference to the speeds maintained. Taken

all round the 5.5 pm up was the harder of the two trains, because it carried a slip coach for Reading, and that entailed slowing down to enter and leave the up main platform line. It took about 2 min more than a clear unchecked run through on the main line. Summary details of six runs on the 5.5 pm are shown on page 72.

The only train that appreciably exceeded the

GWR 11.5 am Paddington-Birmingham

Run no:			1	2	3	4	5	6
Engine no:			2977	2928	103	2916	2977	2929
Engine name:			*Robertson*	*Saint Sebastian*	*President*	*Saint Benedict*	*Robertson*	*Saint Cuthbert*
Load (tons)								
—to Leamington:			275	275	305	305	340	340
—to Birmingham:			250	245	275	245	280	—

Distance miles		Schedule min	Actual m s	Actual m s	Actual m s	Actual m s	Actual m s	Actual m s
0.0	PADDINGTON	0	0 00	0 00	0 00	0 00	0 00	0 00
—			—	signals	—	—	—	—
$3\frac{1}{4}$	*Old Oak West Junction*	6	6 06	7 47	6 40	6 10	6 24	6 05
$7\frac{3}{4}$	Greenford	11	11 50	13 50	12 30	11 32	12 30	11 50
14	*Milepost $3\frac{3}{4}$*		18 04	19 54	18 40	17 42	19 02	18 35
21	*Summit Post $10\frac{3}{4}$*		25 25	27 11	26 26	25 01	26 45	26 39
$21\frac{3}{4}$	Beaconsfield		26 10	27 57	27 15	25 48	27 30	27 28
$26\frac{1}{2}$	HIGH WYCOMBE	30	30 40	32 25	31 55	30 20	32 05	32 05
$28\frac{3}{4}$	West Wycombe		33 45	36 05	35 10	33 20	35 15	35 15
33	*Summit Post $22\frac{3}{4}$*		39 00	41 23	40 37	38 28	41 01	40 36
$34\frac{3}{4}$	Princes Risborough	40	40 45	43 03	42 24	40 15	42 50	42 22
—			—	pw slack	—	pw slack	—	—
$44\frac{1}{4}$	*Ashendon Junction*	50	48 28	52 34	50 05	48 49	50 45	50 01
$51\frac{3}{4}$	*Milepost $7\frac{1}{2}$*		55 10	59 24	57 46	56 42	57 32	56 48
$53\frac{3}{8}$	Bicester	60	56 55	60 55	59 30	58 35	59 15	58 35
$57\frac{1}{4}$	*Summit Post 13*		61 01	64 17	63 36	63 13	63 23	62 54
$62\frac{1}{2}$	*Aynho Junction*	69	66 25	69 07	69 03	68 38	68 48	68 30
—			—	signals	—	—	—	—
$67\frac{1}{2}$	BANBURY	74	71 30	74 35	74 25	73 35	73 48	73 40
$73\frac{1}{4}$	*Milepost 92*		77 40	82 03	80 39	79 33	80 05	79 48
—			—	—	pw slack	signals	—	pw slack
$87\frac{3}{8}$	LEAMINGTON	94	91 00	94 20	95 20	95 30	92 50	94 55
$88\frac{1}{4}$	*Milepost 107*		92 13	95 28	96 35	96 45	94 05	—
$93\frac{1}{4}$	*Summit Post 112*		99 18	pw slack	103 11	102 53	100 46	arrival
$103\frac{1}{2}$	Solihull		111 25	115 17	114 27	113 05	112 15	by slip
$107\frac{1}{4}$	Tyseley		114 50	118 20	118 17	116 10	115 35	coach
—			signals	—	signals	—	—	—
$110\frac{1}{2}$	SNOW HILL	120	120 30	122 20	122 37	120 28	119 35	—
	Net times (min)		$119\frac{1}{2}$	$114\frac{1}{4}$	120	116	$119\frac{1}{2}$	93

Engine No 2901 Lady Superior, *as later equipped with the standard Swindon No 3 superheater.*

GWR 11.5 am Paddington-Birmingham: analysis of uphill performance

Run no:	1	2	3	4	5	6
Engine no:	2977	2928	103*	2916	2977	2919
Engine name:	Robertson	Saint Sebastian	President	Saint Benedict	Robertson	Saint Cuthbert
Load (tons):	275	275	305	305	340	340
Gerrards Cross bank						
Gradient 1 in	264	264	264	264	264	264
Speed (mph)	55½	54	51	53	53½	50
EDHP	920	885	897	947	1045	945
West Wycombe						
Gradient 1 in	164	164	164	164	164	164
Speed (mph)	48½	50½	50	50	44½	48
EDHP	995	1050	1147	1147	1080	1190
Bicester bank						
Gradient 1 in	200	200	200	200	200	200
Speed (mph)	50½	62	51½	47½	50½	47½
EDHP	925	1218	1053	945	1120	1030

*de Glehn four-cylinder compound 4-4-2

level 2 hours was the third, which was stopped dead for 3½ min at one of the automatic signals near Tilehurst, and lost 7¼ min in consequence.

So far as locomotive performance was concerned, by far the finest was that of the first run with *Peveril of the Peak*, when the heavy load of 360 tons was conveyed. The engine had by then been superheated. A little time was lost on the sharp initial timing of 9 min to Filton Junction, which was computed for a train of at least 100 tons less weight. But once round the curve and on to the South Wales main line the performance was splendid. Actually there was very little difference between the two runs with this

engine as far as Didcot, because the average speeds over the 62 miles between Mileposts 112 and 50 were 64.7 and 64.5 mph, with maximum speeds of around 75 mph in both cases, both on the descent from Badminton, and approaching Didcot. But after Didcot, on the second run, the driver began to ease off a little, beginning to draw slightly ahead of time, whereas on the first, having left Bristol 4½ min late, he was continuing to go hard to try and secure a punctual arrival in London. This he would almost have succeeded in doing but for a slight signal check at Old Oak Common.

As more of the four-cylinder 4-6-0s were built it seemed to be the policy of Locomotive

Up Bristol Express near Hayes: engine No 2929 Saint Stephen.

5.5 pm Bristol-Paddington

Engine no:	2917	2986	2921	2941	2985	2985
Engine name:	*Saint Bernard*	*Robin Hood*	*Saint Dunstan*	*Easton Court*	*Peveril of the Peak*	*Peveril of the Peak*
Load (tons)						
—to Reading:	185	205	220	275	360	360
—to Paddington:	160	160	195	240	335	335
Total time (min/sec)	114 37	120 02	122 35	119 40	116 15	118 32
Net time (min)	114	118¼	115	118	115¾	118½

Department headquarters at Swindon to use these engines to the exclusion of all others on the London-West of England expresses via Westbury, and to make increasing use of them on the Birmingham route. When living at Mortimer and, from 1913, travelling daily to school in Reading I cannot recall having seen any but four-cylinder engines on the two expresses which then came regularly within my ken, namely the up Cornish Riviera, and the 3.30 pm down. At the same time, many of the reports of running do not show the spirit of enterprise that came later to characterise the daily work of the four-cylinder engines and their crews.

There was an occasion in 1910 on the 11.0 am West of England express, which began with a non-stop run to Bristol in 2 hours. One of the 'King' series, hauling a load of 345 tons, was stopped by signal no farther from Paddington than Ladbroke Grove box, 1.9 miles. In consequence, the train was 4½ min late passing Southall, and thus it remained, without any further checks all the way to Bristol. But Temple Meads station did their work very smartly, including the addition of extra coaches, and changing engines, and cut their allotted 10 min to 5¾ min, sending the express away on time.

The fresh engine was an 'Atlantic', No 172 *The Abbot*, and with a substantial load of 385 tons a splendid run was made to Exeter. No stop watch readings of speed were taken, but the fine work on the level road to Taunton can be assessed from the averages from point to point set out in the table. One coach was slipped at Taunton, and although from the average speed it is likely that the minimum at Whiteball summit was a little less than 30 mph, this was good work with the reduced load of 350 tons. Another coach was slipped at Tiverton Junction, and it is evident that some very fast running was made descending towards Exeter. Speed was eased round the curves between Cullompton and Hele, and after Silverton there came a final dash, to

Engine No 2936 Cefntilla Court *in plain wartime green* (the late W.J. Reynolds).

reach Exeter 3½ min early, a striking contrast to the lack-lustre quality of the running between Paddington and Bristol. The maximum speeds would have been at least 85 mph at Cullompton, and 80 mph at Stoke Canon. In amplification of this fine performance it should be added that the engine No 172, had recently been superheated, while remaining an 'Atlantic', and was clearly in first class condition. ,

GWR 1.10 pm Bristol-Exeter (in 1910)

Load
—to Taunton: 365 tons tare, 385 tons full
—to Tiverton Junction; 332 tons tare, 350 tons full
—to Exeter: 299 tons tare, 315 tons full
Engine: 4-4-2 No 172 *The Abbot*

Distance miles		Schedule min	Actual m s	Average speed mph
0.0	BRISTOL			
	(TEMPLE MEADS)	0	0 00	—
1.05	Bedminster		3 38	—
5.9	Flax Bourton		10 18	43.7
8.05	Nailsea		12 21	63.0
12.0	Yatton		15 45	69.6
15.6	Puxton		18 56	67.8
19.7	*Uphill Junction*	24	22 43	65.2
24.2	Brent Knoll		26 55	64.3
26.9	Highbridge		29 24	65.2
30.7	Dunball		33 01	63.0
33.25	BRIDGWATER		35 36	59.5
39.8	*Cogload Junction*		42 23	58.2
44.8	TAUNTON (SLIP)	49	47 25	59.7
46.8	Norton Fitzwarren		49 35	55.5
51.9	Wellington		54 43	59.6
55.65	*Whiteball Box*		60 28	39.2
60.7	Tiverton Junction			
	(Slip)		65 26	61.1
63.05	Cullompton		67 07	83.4
67.2	Hele		70 34	72.0
72.15	Stoke Canon		74 35	74.0
75.6	EXETER			
	(ST DAVIDS)	83	79 31	—

Another run of that period, on the 5.45 pm express from Birmingham to Paddington, recalls an interesting service whereby this train was diverted from the direct line from Greenford to make a passenger stop at Ealing Broadway. The run of 83 miles from Leamington was scheduled in 87 min start to stop. As with many of the trains on the new short route to Birmingham, the loads were usually very light, and on one recorded occasion engine No 2914 *Saint Augustine*, by that time superheated, had a load of no more than 186 tons tare on leaving Leamington. A signal check at Banbury caused a loss of 2

min, but the sectional times onwards to Greenford were not improved upon, and the overall time to Ealing Broadway was 87¼ min. At that period it seemed inevitable for express trains to be heavily delayed at Old Oak Common, and this was no exception. It took 14 min to cover the last 5.7 miles into Paddington, start to stop.

My earlier references to the exceptionally fast running of the engine *Saint Bartholomew* on an up Birmingham express have an interesting echo in two runs made in May 1915 on the 12.15 pm express from Banbury to Paddington, both showing a curious inconsistency of effort, reflecting far more, in all probability, the work of the enginemen than the capacity of the locomotive. Both runs were made with engines of the 'Court' series. With trifling loads of 160 tons on the first occasion and only 140 tons on the second, schedule time was 71 min for the non-stop run of 67.5 miles from Banbury. Engine No 2939 *Croome Court* was leaving nearly 12 min late, while No 2933 *Bibury Court* was 10½ min late. With such loads one might have thought it not difficult to recover practically all this lateness. Quite apart from downhill speed the proven tractive capacity of these locomotives would have been enough to mount the adverse gradients at almost any speed desired, and both drivers started away from Banbury as if they meant to be in Paddington on time, or very near it. The comparative times as far as Ashedon Junction were thus:

Engine no		2939	2933
Load (tons)		160	140
Distance miles		Time m s	Time m s
0.0	Banbury	0 00	0 00
5.0	Aynho Junction	6 30	6 13
10.25	Ardley	11 03	10 59
14.1	Bicester	13 54	13 56
17.1	Blackthorn	15 55	16 05
20.1	Brill	18 06	18 17
23.4	Ashendon Junction	21 00	21 12
Average speed (mph)			
	Bicester to Brill	85.7	82.9
Maximum speed (mph) near			
	Blackthorn	90	86

After those very energetic starts, and speeds on the part of *Croome Court* that supported an almost certain 90 mph at Blackthorn, it seemed as though both drivers eased their engines so markedly as to suggest that they were deliberately refraining from regaining any lost time. Both runs were logged by that

Up Birmingham and North express near Gerrards Cross: engine No 2949 Stanford Court.

most expert and erudite of observers R.E. Charlewood, and on the first of the two, after that terrific spurt from Ardley to Ashendon Junction he clocked every milepost from High Wycombe in the natural expectation of getting a very fast descent of the Gerrards Cross bank. Alas for such hopes, for after making a very slow recovery up to Beaconsfield, the driver ran practically without steam, and from Milepost 11 the next eight miles of racing descent, where *Saint Bartholomew* had given Cecil J. Allen a 90 mph, actually took 7 min 12 sec, an average of only 66.7 mph with a maximum of 70½ mph, and after an easing over Ruislip troughs they dawdled on to take 9¼ min over the 10.1 miles to Park Royal. The average speed of only 66 mph from Beaconsfield to this latter station makes a dismal contrast to the lightning work earlier in the journey. One wonders if the driver sensed that some part of the motion was tending to run hot, and eased down deliberately. For once the finish was completely unchecked and Paddington was reached in 69½ min from Banbury.

Charlewood logged the same train a week later with *Bibury Court*, and an even lighter load of 140 tons. The work was very similar, except that this second driver began easing down immediately after passing Ashendon Junction. In relation to the load, the work up the Princes Risborough bank was quite inferior. In later years I myself clocked another engine of the class, with a load of 200 tons to make considerably faster time between Haddenham and High Wycombe. On the second of Mr Charlewood's runs *Bibury Court*

was taken down the Gerrards Cross bank rather more vigorously, though not exceeding 78 mph. Because of the faster running from High Wycombe, he would have regained 3½ min of the 10½ min late start from Banbury, but there were signal delays at Park Royal. Light though the loads were on these two occasions, the runs are important as showing that, contrary to what is sometimes believed, the 'Saint' Class could attain high maximum speeds in favourable conditions. That they were not very kind to the track when doing so was shown some years later during the investigations of the Bridge Street Committee. So far as cab comfort was concerned, in my own footplate work I found considerable variation between individual engines, with one of the 'Courts' giving a very smooth ride at speeds approaching 80 mph.

Now, in the most complete contrast to these Birmingham route runs, and to bring the pre-1917 era to a close, there is a trip on the down Cornish Riviera Express, whereon No 2943 *Hampton Court* took a tremendous load of no less than 535 tons out of Paddington. The date was 1912, in the height of the summer holiday season, and then the 'Saints' had not been entirely displaced from the crack Paddington-Plymouth working. The driver was a Laira man, Nork by name, who usually had the four-cylinder engine *Knight of the Garter*, and gave Mr Dunn some good runs with it, but before the days of the 'Castles' I have seen nothing to approach let alone surpass the extraordinary work he got out of No 2943 on that summer holiday day in July. On the last day of the 1925 Interchange Trials between the 'Castles' and the LNER Gresley 'Pacifics', when the driver of No 4074 *Caldicot Castle*, was under instructions to go as hard as he could, and make a spectacular run, he took 37 min 25 sec to cover the 36 miles to Reading. On the journey Mr Dunn logged in 1912, *Hampton Court* passed Reading in 13 sec faster time.

The comparative times from Paddington, with the same load make remarkable reading:

Engine name		*Hampton Court*	*Caldicot Castle*
Distance		**Time**	**Time**
miles		**m s**	**m s**
0.0	Paddington	0 00	0 00
9.1	Southall	12 09	12 42
18.5	Slough	20 41	21 26
24.2	Maidenhead	25 48	26 36
31.0	Twyford	31 50	32 49
36.0	Reading (pass)	37 12	37 25

Hampton Court was thus leading by a minute at Twyford, and the difference thereafter was that in 1912 the speed restriction at Reading for trains turning on to the Berks and Hants line was right down to 15 mph whereas *Caldicot Castle* was able to take the junction at only a little less than 50 mph. This gave the 'Castle' a much better start up the Kennet Valley, and an advantage of 1¾ min in passing Newbury. Allowing for this, however, the two engines were running 'neck and neck' as it were right up to Savernake summit, with the 17 miles between Newbury and the last mentioned station taking 17 min 50 sec (by No 2943) and 17 min 47 sec (by No 4074). Seeing that the respective tractive efforts of the two locomotives were 24,395 and 31,626 lb (a 30 per cent advantage to the 'Castle') and that the latter engine was going specially hard by instruction, this was a remarkable exposition as to the extent that *Hampton Court* was being opened out.

After that the comparison ceases, because the latter engine was justifiably eased on the descent to Westbury, not exceeding 72 mph, whereas the 'Castle' went like the wind! Details of the Savernake ascent by *Hampton Court* make astonishing reading, thus:

	Average speed mph
Mileposts 41 to 47	58
Mileposts 47 to 50	56
Mileposts 50 to 59	60

and the last five miles of the climb were run at 58, 57.2, 54.5, 50 and 45.5 mph.

Only one coach was slipped at Westbury, and *Hampton Court* continued with a gross load of 500 tons. At that time also the train had to pass Frome at much reduced speed, and magnificent work was done in accelerating this great train, and covering the 7.2 miles up to the Milepost 122¾ summit in 9 min 20 sec. With a fast descent of the Bruton bank, and a top speed of 77 mph, Castle Cary was passed exactly on time in 121 min for the 115.3 miles from Paddington. Having regard to the severe speed restrictions at Reading, Westbury and Frome, this was a truly superlative achievement, and must be reckoned alongside that of·the *Saint Vincent*, between Paddington and Bath, as described in Chapter 5 as among the finest ever with the 'Saint' Class locomotives. In comparing the run of *Hampton Court* with more recent performances over the West of England main line, the 15 mph restriction at Reading must be considered as worth about 2 min extra, while the elimination of the Westbury and Frome slacks consequent upon construction of the by-pass lines, with no corresponding restrictions in speed, meant a further saving of about 4 min. Thus in relation to running conditions in the 1930s and later, this wonderful run was equivalent to a post-war run through Castle Cary in about 115 min, or an average of 60 mph from the start at Paddington. This unfortunately was the end of fast running.

At Cogload Junction the train became involved in the congestion of holiday traffic from the north, a stop was called for on the goods avoiding line at Taunton, and a pilot was taken up to Whiteball summit, where a further stop was made to detach this engine. It took 193½ min to pass Exeter, where the load was reduced from 434 to 343 tons tare, and a further stop was necessary for assistance over the South Devon banks. Eventually Plymouth was reached 21½ min late. This was no fault of engine, or crew. An analysis of the performance out to Savernake gives remarkable results. On the level and faintly rising line between Paddington and Reading the drawbar pull was sustained at about 3¼ tons for 20 miles, while after recovery from the slacks over the Reading junction, in making an average speed of 59 mph over the 26 miles between Posts 41 and 67, on an average rising gradient of 1 in 500, the drawbar pull was nearly 3¾ tons, equal to a drawbar horsepower of about 1300. Apart from the brief intermission through Reading this effort had been sustained for the first 70 min of the journey to Plymouth.

Chapter 8

Redeployment of the 'Saints'

At the beginning of 1913 an order for a further ten engines of the 'Court' series was issued to Swindon Works, but largely because of strong representations made by the locomotive running inspectors, to whom Churchward always lent a most sympathetic ear, the order was subsequently curtailed to five, engines 2951-5, and the remaining five 4-6-0 engines for which financial provision had been made were built as four-cylinder 'Star' Class. The inspectors, while appreciating to the full the admirable qualities of the 'Saint' Class, considered that on a long through run with a heavy train the 'Stars' were 'one coach better'.

In the following year, a further 15 'Stars' were built at Swindon bringing their total up to 61. With the 'Stars' taking almost complete possession of the West of England service, and also of the Birmingham and North trains via Bicester, between Paddington and Wolver-hampton, many of the 'Saints' were moved to areas not previously favoured with 4-6-0 loco-motives. This was very appropriate in many cases because the nature of the roads made the

noted hill-climbing capacity of the two-cylinder engines especially welcome.

There is no doubt that in general the 'Stars' were more comfortable engines to ride. One did not experience the constant vibration that was often present on the 'Saints', especially when they were pulled up inside about 25 per cent cut-off, and while I would not suggest that the views of the corps of running inspectors had been influenced by anything so mundane as 'creature comfort' there was also the fact that the nominal tractive effort of the latest variety of 'Star', having 15 in diameter cylinders, was some 14 per cent greater than that of the 'Saints'. Despite this, there were some very successful drivers in that most *élite* of Great Western links, the No 1 at Wolverhampton, who preferred the smaller-cylindered 'Stars'. The relative merits of the 'Saints' and 'Stars' in another respect came into prominence during the researches of the Bridge Stress Committee, set up in 1919 by the Government of the day, to review the methods of calculating the stresses in bridges,

The French Compound La France *as fitted with GWR standard No 1 superheated boiler* (the late M.W. Earley).

with particular reference to the allowances to be made for impact, as distinct from dead weight loading. It was an investigation that revealed a wide diversity of practice on the British railways, and some glaring inconsistencies in the methods used even within the precincts of the same drawing office. The fact that a locomotive gave its crew a smooth and comfortable ride, even at the highest speeds, did not necessarily mean that it was kind to the track—sometimes very much the reverse.

Until the time of the Bridge Stress Committee investigations with the four-cylinder 'Stars' it had been the practice at Swindon to balance a proportion of the reciprocating parts separately for the inside and outside cylinders, in the leading and middle pairs of coupled wheels respectively. This followed the practice of some other establishments with four-coupled inside cylinder locomotives which put the entire balance for the reciprocating parts into the leading coupled axle, with murderous effects on the track!

In the original scheme of balancing for the 'Stars', although the balance applied to the leading coupled wheels was opposed to that on the middle pair, and the total effect was relatively small, the 'dynamic augment' to the dead weight on the axles, when the engine was running at high speed, was very severe, far worse than on the two-cylinder 'Saint'. Because of the interaction between the two sets of balancing on the 'Stars', however, the engines themselves worked very smoothly and no one suspected what they were doing to the track! Then, in 1924, with the ingenious measuring equipment of the Bridge Stress Committee installed to record what happened, engines of both classes were driven at high speed across the viaduct over the River Parrett, at Langport, Somerset. This is an N-girder through bridge of 112 ft span, and lying at the foot of the 1 in 264 gradient from Somerton Tunnel was a place where a high speed could quickly be worked up. Both engines were running light.

The first set of deflection diagrams horrified Swindon. There was nothing much that could be done about the 'Saint', which it turned out was far better than that of some other two-cylinder 4-6-0s which were tested, but the design of the balancing of the 'Stars' was redesigned, linking the two hitherto independent mechanisms in such a way that the individual wheel effect, and the total combined axle load was quite sensationally

reduced. The committee had decided to fix the 'hammer blow' effect, for comparative purposes, at a wheel speed of six revolutions per second, which in the case of the Great Western 4-6-0s meant 86 mph and at that speed the revised figures were:

Engine class	Max axle load tons	Speed mph	Hammerblow Whole engine tons	Axle tons	Max combined load tons
'Saint'	18.4	86	17.9	6.9	25.3
'Star'	18.6	86	3.7	3.7	21.5

By way of comparison the maximum combined axle loading at a speed of six revolutions per second for certain other well known British express locomotives may be quoted as follows:

Railway	Engine class	Type	Maximum combined axle load tons
Southern	'King Arthur'	4-6-0	28.6
Midland	Class '2P' super	4-4-0	29.3
Great Northern	'251'	4-4-2	30.4
Caledonian	'60' Class	4-6-0	31.0

Even so, with no more than 25.3 tons, the 'Saint' produced some fairly strong vertical oscillations on that bridge at Langport.

After the construction of the 'Princess' series of 'Stars' in 1914, and the redistribution of the 4-6-0 stud in consequence one of the largest concentration of 'Saints' was at Bristol, where until the later 1920s, they had no other 4-6-0s. There, of course, they continued with workings on which they had been used, almost from the start, such as the 2-hour London trains, but some of the more interesting developments took place elsewhere.

It was during the First World War that Worcester received its first 4-6-0 locomotives. There were two non-stop expresses down from Paddington, the 1.40 pm slipping coaches at Kingham, took 135 min for the 120.5 mile run, while the 4.45 pm, which was 5 min faster to Worcester, slipped a coach at Moreton-in-Marsh. In pre-war days these were fairly light trains, not infrequently worked by single-wheelers. In my boyhood at Reading I used to see the 8.55 am up from Worcester come tearing through, always hauled by an inside cylinder 4-4-0, a 'City' or an 'Atbara'. Only one of the Worcester down non-stops was reintroduced after the war, first leaving Paddington at 1.30 pm and then at

Above *Engine No 2927* Saint Patrick *as restored to pre-war style of painting* (the late W.J. Reynolds).

Below *The historic* Albion, *as superheated with No 1 standard boiler, working up West of England express with through NBR coaches for Aberdeen, descending Dainton bank* (R. Brookman).

12.45. The timing from the winter of 1921 was 130 min, but the non-stop was not reinstated following the cancellations after the General Strike of 1926.

The 'Saints' were excellent engines for the Worcester line, which included, in the up direction, the severe climb from Honeybourne, in the Vale of Evesham, up to Chipping Campden, high in the Cotswolds, 4½ miles continuously at 1 in 100, preceeded by nearly a mile at 1 in 126. The alignment, however, is magnificently straight, so much so that in later years several unofficial attempts at a new speed record were made, by 'Castle' Class engines. In pre-war years A.V. Goodyear logged no higher maximum than 78½ mph, and that with a 4-2-2 single, but after the train was restored in 1921 he had one instance of a 5-mile stretch past Honeybourne being covered in 3 min 47 sec, an average of 79.5 mph and a maximum of 84 mph. The engine was No 2985 *Peveril of the Peak*, which I used to see frequently at Paddington on the Worcester trains. The train then took a 12-coach load out of Paddington, slipped two coaches at Kingham and another one at Evesham. The coaches slipped at Kingham went forward to Cheltenham, and provided a service from London, via Andoversford and Charlton Kings, nearly as rapid as that by the Cheltenham Spa Express, via Swindon and Gloucester.

Another shed at which an influx of 'Saints' was especially welcome in the war years was Shrewsbury, for use on the West to North trains via the Severn Tunnel. Hitherto the largest Great Western engines available had been the 4-4-0 outside cylindered 'Counties', which on that route did some of their finest work. I shall always associate the use of these engines, and of the 'Saints' too, on that line with an amusing contribution made by Sir William Stanier, to the discussion on a paper read by K.J. Cook before the Institution of Locomotive Engineers. It did show how very eminent men can get mixed up when it comes to reminiscing! Stanier said: 'Mr Cook has drawn attention to the 4-4-0 'County' Class engine. Churchward had built that engine with his tongue in his cheek. He knew the front end was too powerful for the wheel base. This engine was built for working trains on the Shrewsbury and Hereford line, which was a joint line with the L & NW, and the L & NW objected at that time to the 4-6-0 'Saint' Class working over it. He was not going to be told what he could do by old Webb! Therefore

Churchward built the 'County' which had plenty of power to run the service.'

Actually, Webb had retired in the early spring of 1903 from his tenure of office as Chief Mechanical Engineer of the LNWR, and if there had been any case of veto, it would have been the Civil Engineer, and not he who would exercise it. In any case it was many years after the 'Counties' had been introduced before any 'Saints' could be spared for the West to North route, but it made a good story in Stanier's jovial way of putting it across in discussion.

When a number of them were allocated to the Coleham sheds at Shrewsbury it was in the realisation that for the physical characteristics of that route they were ideal. With heavy loads, heavy gradients and little opportunity for sustained fast running, their two-cylinder engine layout and the Churchward arrangement of the Stephenson link motion gave them a capacity for uphill performance which their more elegant sister-engines of the 'Star' Class seemed unable to equal. The Salop engines were of course also available for working southwards to Wolverhampton and northward to Chester, though on the latter section at first loads were so relatively light that 4-4-0s could do all that was necessary.

South Wales was also a happy hunting ground for the 'Saints'. In addition to Canton shed, Cardiff, there was quite a concentration of them at Landore (Swansea), where in later years many of them earned particular fame in working the London expresses on the double-home turns to Paddington. When, before the First World War, attempts were being made to develop Fishguard as an ocean terminal, as well as a packet station for the Irish service, there were thoughts of non-stop running from Paddington with the American boat trains, and there were occasional workings of the 'Star' Class engines but as the service settled down into a purely Irish business the running of the boat trains devolved upon Landore shed.

The route beyond Swansea is a curious mixture of level and very severe grading. At first there comes the Cockett 'gable', inclined at 1 in 50 in both directions, followed by 27 miles of virtually level road round the coast to the Carmarthen avoiding line. The last 15 miles into Fishguard includes much sharp grading, severe curvature and finally a precipitous single-tracked descent into Fishguard itself. The mail train leaving Swansea at midnight called only at Llanelly, and in view of the various restrictions did well to run the 62 miles to Fishguard in 77 min. The corresponding inward bound train leaving Fishguard at 3.55 am ran the 72.7 miles to Swansea non-stop in 98 min. I cannot recall having seen any detailed timings of the running of these trains.

The redeployment of the 4-6-0 locomotive stud following the construction of the final batch of 'Stars', in 1914, saw a marked reduction in the importance of Exeter as a main line locomotive centre, in favour of Newton Abbot. It was, of course, always a sub-depot, responsible to the Divisional Locomotive Carriage and Wagon Superintendent at Newton Abbot, but a number of the long distance express trains changed engines at Exeter, and many of the locomotives illustrated in this book were posed for their portraits with the high west wall and all-over roof of St Davids station as a background. But Exeter shed retained at least one prestigious mainline working well into the 1920s, nearly always powered by 'Saint' Class engines. This was the West of England postal special, over the entire distance between Paddington and Penzance, via Bristol. An Exeter engine worked the up train, leaving Penzance at 6 pm through to Paddington, being remanned at Exeter. The men lodged at Old Oak, and then returned on the corresponding down train, on

which engines as well as crews were changed at Exeter.

Unlike its famous counterpart between Euston and Aberdeen, this train carried no passenger section at any part of its journeys to and from the west. I saw it frequently when I was on holiday in Cornwall in 1924, and engines that I recall seeing frequently on the duty were 2906 *Lady of Lynn*, 2910 *Lady of Shalott*, 2917 *Saint Bernard*, 2937 *Clevedon Court* and 2978 *Kirkland*. They arrived in the early morning, and spent most of the day tucked away in the back of the shed at Penzance.

The Exeter 'Saints' had another important duty in the early 1920s, on the up Cornish Riviera Express, between Truro and Plymouth. At that time 'The Limited' used to change engines in both directions at Truro. Westbound one Penzance engine and its crew used to relieve another, with those who had worked down from Plymouth going forward to Penzance on a succeeding stopping train. The engines were always 2-6-0s of the '53XX' series. The other 'Saint' Class engines that worked regularly into the West Country were those from Bath Road shed, Bristol. They had an almost complete monopoly of the West to North trains, as far as Plymouth, and equally of the service from the west to Birmingham and Wolverhampton when that was restored after

The up West of England postal train leaving Penzance in 1924, hauled by engine No 2937 Clevedon Court.

the war. On this, however, the 'Saints' worked no farther north than Bristol, because the LMS would not then allow them to use the line between Yate and Standish Junction, over which the GWR had running powers.

In writing of post-war developments in the West Country I have drawn somewhat ahead of true chronological sequence, for I have not yet made any detailed reference to the important war service rendered by the 'Saint' Class engines on the West to North route via the Severn Tunnel. When the last batch of 'Counties' was built at Swindon in 1911, eight out of the ten were allocated to the North to West service, with Bath Road and Salop shed getting four each. But in the redeployment of the 'Saints', after 1914, Bath Road acquired more of them, and some of these, in partnership with the 'Saints' newly allocated to Salop, were able to take over most of the West to North service from 1916 onwards.

The route itself was an extremely difficult one. It was not only the actual inclination of the worst banks, but that so many of them are preceeded by curves needing a drastic reduction of speed, or include tunnels in which the atmosphere is conducive to slipping. The section between Bristol and Pontypool Road could have been the worst of all with the single line tunnels at Patchway in addition to the Severn Tunnel itself, and the slow negotiation of the Maindee junctions outside Newport as a prelude to the toilsome climb up to Pontypool Road. When the 'Counties' were holding the fort, however, in pre-war years the loading was much lighter, and the attaching or detaching of through sections of the train for South Wales at Pontypool Road often reduced the tonnage to be hauled by the through engine by 100 tons or so, on the difficult stretch through the Severn Tunnel.

The loads were often heaviest between Pontypool Road and Hereford, because at the latter station one or more coaches might be detached for working through to Worcester and Birmingham, via Great Malvern. Furthermore, in cases of exceptional loading the train engines were often piloted between Hereford and Pontypool Road, using 4-4-0s of the inside-cylindered 'Bulldog' Class. It is nevertheless important to appreciate that despite the very great increase in train loadings, due to war conditions, little if any relaxation of schedule times was made. By comparison with the fast pre-war schedules that were operating on the main lines radiating from London, so far as booked average speeds were concerned, these were not spectacular, though they involved hard collar-

5.30 am Paddington–Penzance express climbing Rattery Incline, Engine No 2922 Saint Gabriel *assisted by 2-6-2 tank No 3121 (O.S. Nock).*

The French compound Alliance *fitted with GWR standard No 1 superheated boiler* (the late M.W. Earley).

work when loads exceeded 400 tons behind the tender. In all cases engines were changed at Bristol. The practice of through locomotive working between Newton Abbot and Shrewsbury on certain trains did not begin until many years later.

Two runs with relatively light loads will make a useful introduction to this route, on which trains of 275 and 280 tons were taken north from Pontypool Road by engines 2954, *Tockenham Court*, and 2924, *Saint Helena*. The gradients are favourable from the start to the crossing of the River Usk at Penpergwm, and speeds rose quickly to 64 and 62½ mph respectively before reductions to 55 and 49½ mph round the curve over the viaduct. These reductions made a bad start to the climb up to Llanvihangel, beside the spectacular Sugar Loaf Mountain. This 6.7 miles of ascent begins with three at 1 in 154, and finishes with nearly four at 1 in 82-95.

Tockenham Court did the better work, taking exactly 11 min over this adverse stretch and not falling below 30 mph. *Saint Helena*, from a lower initial speed, fell to 25½ mph at one point and took 12¾ min, but followed with some faster downhill running towards Hereford. Here the maximum speed was 72½ mph, against 64 on the first run, so catching up on overall time, and reaching Hereford punctually in 45 min from Pontypool Road, 33.4 miles. *Tockenham Court*, despite the relatively slow running after Llanvihangel, finished in 44½ min.

From Hereford northwards details are available of four runs with 'Saint' Class engines on which much heavier loads were conveyed, and

for easy reference the running times are tabulated.

The first of the four runs is the continuation from Hereford of that with *Tockenham Court* just mentioned, on which, by a unusual inversion of the normal traffic arrangements, the train load was increased. The other three were wartime occasions on which very heavy loads were conveyed. So far as the road itself is concerned, although there are intermediate fluctuations, the general tendency is continuously adverse from Hereford right up to Church Stretton. The average inclination is not more than about 1 in 600 for the first 29 miles, but after that the average is about 1 in 200 to the summit point just short of Church Stretton station.

To cover this stretch of 38.2 miles, the express train timings allowed 47 to 48 min and involved an average speed of 50 mph up from Leominster. The descent into Shrewsbury is continuous and steep from Church Stretton, but, with much curvature, speeds are not usually very high. To maintain an average speed of 48 mph over such a road with loads exceeding 400 tons involved some of the finest locomotive work demanded of any Great Western engines in the later years of the First World War.

Tockenham Court, with no more than 350 tons, had a relatively easy task, and beyond a good start out of Hereford did work that was no more than moderate until the final ascent to Church Stretton. After an initial maximum speed of 58½ mph, the fluctuations in the rising gradients to Craven Arms were taken with speed variations between 45 and 61 mph, but the final section on gradients of 1 in 104-112 was climbed with the excellent minimum speed of 38 mph. The entire 30.7 miles of climbing from Dinmore to Church Stretton was covered at an average speed of exactly 50 mph. The steep descent to Shrewsbury was taken with commendable wartime economy, almost entirely without steam, and not exceeding 60 mph anywhere, to complete the journey comfortably within the 65 min then allowed to this train. *Tockenham Court* was then a Bristol engine.

On the next run, *Lady of Lyons*, which already has a notable record of performance in this book alone, was one of the engines transferred from the West Country to Salop, and was at that shed, so far as I can trace, for the rest of her existence. She was in characteristically excellent form on this run, drawing ahead of *Tockenham Court* by nearly 2 min by Craven Arms. The record presented to me does not include any maximum and minimum speeds, but the station to station averages give an impressive picture of the work being performed, such as 57.7 mph from Dinmore to Leominster, 59.2 on to Woofferton Junction, 56.7 to Ludlow, and 51.5 to Craven Arms. This latter was a remarkable average seeing that it included the recovery from the usual slack to about 45 mph round the curve at Ludlow, and the first taste of the steeper climbing with 1½ miles of 1 in 112 before Craven Arms. On the final ascent the time fell a little behind that of *Tockenham Court*, after which there followed an equally gentle descent to Shrewsbury.

The 'star' run of the collection, however, was the third, on which the one-time 'Atlantic' engine No 2983 *Redgauntlet* had to tackle a load of no less than 420 tons. In the early stages the times fell behind those of the previous run to an extent that would be considered justified by the additional load, though in itself representing first class work. The station to station average speeds had thus far been 55.6, 58.1 and 55.2 mph. But then the effort was substantially stepped up, to such an extent that the average speeds were 53.8 mph from Ludlow to Craven Arms, and a remarkable 42.5 mph up the really steep final pitch to Church Stretton. The time was only 10 sec slower than that of *Tockenham Court*, with 70 tons greater load. The average speed of 52 mph for the entire 30.7 miles up from Dinmore was a performance fit to rank with the finest pre-war running of the 'Saint' Class on the West of England road. The descent into Shrewsbury was slower than ever on this trip.

On the fourth journey tabulated, the running of the romantically named *Lalla Rookh*, with an even heavier load, is rather overshadowed by the brilliance of the preceeding one, but an average speed of just 50 mph from Dinmore to Church Stretton with such a load as 425 tons was no mean achievement. The descent to Shrewsbury was slower than ever, which seemed traditional with the Bristol engines and their drivers.

In the southbound direction, details are tabulated of five wartime runs, on trains still having the 'crack' pre-war timing of 63 min from Shrewsbury to Hereford, even though the loads taken unpiloted rose to a maximum of no less than 450 tons. In this direction, with Salop-based engines, the climbing to Church Stretton was not so vigorous as might be expected from the 'Saint' Class, though the

GWR Hereford-Shrewsbury

Run no:		1	2	3	4
Engine no:		2954	2903	2983	2982
Engine name:		Tockenham Court	Lady of Lyons	Redgauntlet	Lalla Rookh
Load (tons gross) behind tender.		350	380	420	425
Distance	**Schedule***	**Actual**	**Actual**	**Actual**	**Actual**
miles	**min**	**m s**	**m s**	**m s**	**m s**
0.0 HEREFORD	0	0 00	0 00	0 00	0 00
7.5 Dinmore		11 00	10 50	11 00	11 40
12.6 Leominster	16	16 35	16 08	16 30	17 12
18.9 Woofferton Junction	3½	23 40	22 31	23 00	23 50
23.5 Ludlow	28	29 00	27 22	28 00	28 40
31.1 Craven Arms	37	38 05	36 15	36 30	37 45
38.2 Church Stretton	47	47 55	46 25	46 30	48 35
51.0 SHREWSBURY	64	64 20	62 49	63 30	65 10

*Runs 2 and 3 only, runs 1 and 4 allowed 65 min.

fact that they were starting 'cold' from Shrewsbury should be taken into account. These no more than moderate initial climbs to Church Stretton were, however, followed by much faster downhill running, war or no war.

That initial bank can be something of a 'killer'. After the sharply curved start past the Coleham engine sheds to Sutton Bridge Junction the gradient is 1 in 127 for nearly two miles. There is a brief easing, for about two miles after Condover station, but then for five miles the upward inclination is continuously between 1 in 90 and 1 in 117. On the five runs tabulated, the average speeds over the last 3½ miles between Leebotwood and Church Stretton were 37.6, 32.4, 33.3, 30.2 and 27.7 mph. The schedule times quoted alongside the actual running times are those of the 63 min booking. On the first run, however, *Lady of Lynn* was working to a 65 min booking and maintained point-to-point more accurately than any of the other engines. The intermediate times scheduled were 21 min to Church Stretton, 37 to Ludlow, and 49 to Leominster.

On this first run, after her vigorous ascent to Church Stretton, *Lady of Lynn* was taken in quite leisurely style down to Hereford, averaging no more than 53.9 mph from Church Stretton to Leominster. The speeds were almost those prescribed by the working times. It was just the reverse on the second run, for after no more than a moderate initial

climb *Lady Macbeth* went downhill as if the furies of Dunsinane were in hot pursuit of her! The maximum speeds of 78 mph before Craven Arms, 72 mph at Woofferton and 69 mph at Moreton were unusually high for any period on this route, let alone for wartime. Her average of 67.5 mph from Craven Arms to Leominster, included a careful slowing round the Ludlow curves. On her second run, *Lady of Lynn* was less vigorous on the ascent to Church Stretton, but began the subsequent descent by touching 75 mph before Craven Arms. After that, however, she was very much eased, and ran placidly forward to arrive in Hereford nearly 3 min early.

The last two runs in the table, with their very heavy loads, included some fine climbing up to Church Stretton. *Saint Helena* would appear to have been notched up on the easier grading from Condover, as her acceleration was slower than usual, but her concluding effort, with its average of 30 mph over the last 3½ miles of ascent was very fine. The subsequent downhill running was leisurely, nevertheless keeping time, though a signal check outside Hereford caused a loss of 2 min in running time.

The last run was a remarkable effort made when the schedule was still at its pre-war 63 min. The train was absolutely packed with passengers, so much so that the gentleman who took the running times could not risk going forward to note the number and name

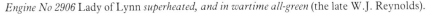

Engine No 2906 Lady of Lynn *superheated, and in wartime all-green* (the late W.J. Reynolds).

of the engine, for fear of losing his seat! He was in the portion for South Wales detached at Pontypool Road, and had no sight of the engine other than a distant view from the rear end of the train when leaving Shrewsbury. So the engine making one of the finest runs of the whole collection, over this route, must remain anonymous. The downhill running from Church Stretton was brisk, though not up to the pace set by *Lady Macbeth* on run No 2.

On the Worcester line, before the 1.40 pm non-stop from Paddington had been cancelled and its working combined with the following 1.45 pm engine, No 2902 *Lady of the Lake* made a run that was typical of some of the working conditions in 1916, with a load of 345 tons. The running was normal at the start, with a maximum speed of 69 mph on the level at Slough and a time of 32¾ min to passing the 30th milepost out of Paddington, but then a long series of signal checks marked the approach to, and passage through Reading. An ambulance train was unloading at the down main platform, a necessarily slow process, and other trains, fast and slow alike, were queuing up to pass through the station on the down slow line.

In view of the humanitarian task in hand, the delay experienced by the Worcester express of only 13 min was small, and once clear of Reading and back on to the fast line the driver of the *Lady of the Lake* quickly stepped up the effort, and was running at 68 mph before the slowing to turn on to the Oxford line at Didcot East Junction. Despite a slight signal check, the train passed Oxford itself, 63½ miles, in 82 min.

Up the steadily rising gradients into the Cotswolds, speed was maintained at little below 60 mph and the slip portion at Kingham, 84.7 miles, was detached in 106¾ min, from Paddington. Descending the Honeybourne bank a maximum speed of 75 mph was attained, but there were signal checks at Littleton and Evesham and eventually Worcester was reached in 144¾ min, 9¾ min late. But allowing for the delays, the net time was no more than 125 min, an average of 57.7 mph. After the detaching of the slip portion at Kingham the load was 255 tons.

I have not, unfortunately, been able to trace any running details of 'Saint' Class performance in climbing the Honeybourne bank, but so far as those engines newly transferred to Worcester were concerned, two runs by No 2908 *Lady of Quality* may be mentioned though going no farther westward than Oxford. Both were on trains booked non-stop in 70 min for the 63½ miles from Paddington, and both, surprisingly enough for 1916, were entirely unchecked. On the first run with a 350-ton load, the first 36 miles to Reading took 38 min, and Didcot East Junction, 53 miles, was passed in 54½ min at a reduced speed of 40 mph. On the second run, with 420 tons, the going was necessarily slower, with corresponding times of 40¼ and 56½ min. The arrival times in Oxford were 68½ and 70 min, both very satisfactory work with substantial trains.

GWR Shrewsbury-Hereford

Run no:		1	2	3	4	5
Engine no:		2906	2905	2906	2924	'Saint'
Engine name:		*Lady of Lynn*	*Lady Macbeth*	*Lady of Lynn*	*Saint Helena*	Class
Load (tons gross) behind tender:		355	360	385	430	450
Distance	Schedule	**Actual**	**Actual**	**Actual**	**Actual**	**Actual**
miles	min	m s	m s	m s	m s	m s
0.0 SHREWSBURY	0	0 00	0 00	0 00	0 00	0 00
4.3 Condover		8 42	8 50	8 55	8 30	8 28
9.3 Leebotwood		14 45	15 45	15 25	15 40	15 05
12.8 Church Stretton	21	20 20	22 13	21 45	22 38	22 42
19.9 Craven Arms	29	—	29 10	28 50	29 30	29 30
27.5 Ludlow	37	36 45	35 17	36 05	37 00	35 55
32.1 Woofferton Junction	42	—	39 40	—	—	40 55
38.4 Leominster	49	48 50	45 37	47 55	49 11	47 15
46.8 Moreton-on-Lugg	—	—	54 10	56 35	signals	56 01
—			signals	—	—	—
51.0 HEREFORD	65	63 36	62 05	62 15	65 40	61 50
Net times (min)		63½	60	62¼	63½	61¾★

★Schedule 63 min.

Chapter 9

The amazing Twenties

The Great Western Railway restored full pre-war standards of speed on all its principal express routes in the autumn of 1921. By that time, no new express passenger locomotives had been built at Swindon, but the series of twelve four-cylinder 'Abbey' 4-6-0s was turned out in 1922, and the first ten 'Castles' came out in the following year. Their introduction did not appreciably affect the allocation or working of the 'Saint' Class engines, except that the allocation of one or two 'Abbeys' to Stafford Road shed, Wolverhampton, marked the final disappearance of 'Saints' from the 2-hour Birmingham trains, except on relief portions at holiday week-ends. The first ten 'Castles' were all stationed at Old Oak Common. It was in the summer of 1923 that the Great Western began its climb towards the railway speed championship of Great Britain, and then the 'Saints', or at least one member of the class, played a prominent part.

The 2.30 pm express from Cheltenham to Paddington was chosen for acceleration, and the 77.3 mile run up from Swindon booked non-stop in 75 min. The margin by which the train became the fastest in the country was by no more than a few decimal points in the average speed, because both the Great Central and the North Eastern then had start-to-stop runs booked at 61.5 mph, against the Great Western's 61.8 mph. But, as we were to learn later, it was only a beginning.

The inaugural run was on July 9 1923, and the selected engine was No 2915 *Saint Bartholomew*. Although in the wartime plain green, with the tapered cast iron chimney, it was beautifully turned out, to begin a highly constrained and cosseted phase of its long life. It will be recalled that in earlier days it clocked up a maximum of 90 mph descending the Gerrards Cross bank, while the final chapter of this book records an astonishing performance under British Railways ownership that gives an additional glitter to the old gentleman's halo. But in July 1923, and for some considerable time thereafter, *Saint Bartholomew* went down to Swindon on a train of milk empties, and returned on the 'Cheltenham Flyer'. It was not until later that the engine worked down to Gloucester on the 10.45 am from Paddington, and prefaced the fast run up from Swindon by some hard pulling through the Cotswold country between Stroud and Sapperton Tunnel.

When it was first accelerated, the 'Flyer' was a considerably heavier train than it afterwards became, and on the inaugural day it carried a nine-coach load, two of which were of the clerestory-roofed type. The gross tonnage behind the tender would have been about 265. The fastest running was between Didcot and Reading with an average speed of 77 mph, and with Slough (58.8 miles) passed nearly 3 min early, in 52¾ min from the start, the engine was eased, to arrive in Paddington nevertheless 3 min before time with a start to stop average speed of 64.5 mph instead of the booked 61.8 mph.

The late Cecil J. Allen travelled by the train shortly afterwards, and, as usual with anything new, went into panegyrics of enthusiasm that were hardly justified by the data he recorded. It was a good run, with an arrival 1½ min early after two slight checks *en route*, and in *The Railway Magazine* of September 1923 he wrote: 'My first experience on the train was so startling in certain of its features as to lead me to the reflection that it would be of little use for the London and North Eastern Railway or any other line to enter into serious competition with the Great Western Railway for the top place in the speed table. With so unique a length of level line, and such unique locomotives to turn it to the best advantage, the Great Western may be said to hold a hand of trumps so far as speed records are concerned'. It must be added that Allen was an LNER man, and after describing his own run, which, with a load lighter by one coach gave a net average speed of 66.2 mph, he rubbed in his conviction still deeper. 'If the Great Western Railway is setting out seriously to capture and retain the blue riband of start-to-stop railway speed, as I remarked previously, in such circumstances as these it would seem idle for any other aspirant so much as attempt to compete!' Good though they were, however, I do not think the 'Saints' were as perfect, or unique as all that, and I just wonder if the attention of the recently appointed Chief Mechanical Engineer of the LNER was ever drawn to that article!

The continuing quality and immense

Above *The inaugural run of the* Cheltenham Flyer, *2.30 pm Cheltenham to Paddington on July 9 1923, near Acton, hauled by engine No 2915* Saint Bartholomew (British Railways).

Below *Bristol to Paddington express passing Sonning box, east of Reading engine No 2949* Stanford Court (the late M.W. Earley).

revenue-earning potential of the 'Saint' Class engines was shown not in the working of light trains like the 'Cheltenham Flyer', which was in any case soon turned over to the four-cylinder engines, but in massive haulage assignments on the South Wales service. Fortunately, this work is very fully and authoritatively documented, but before turning to a new appraisal of it, reference must be made to two runs on the 12 noon up 2-hour Bristol express that put the working of the 'Cheltenham Flyer' completely in the shade. Both were logged by a very experienced recorder, Mr Humphrey Baker, of Bath, and details are set out in the accompanying table. The run up from Bristol begins with the heavy ascent of the Filton bank (1 in 75) and the long pull at 1 in 300

from the top of this incline up to Badminton. Then after the descent to the crossing of the Wiltshire Avon, at Little Somerford comes the corresponding rise to the summit at Milepost 80, which was hindered inter-mediately by the need to reduce speed over the junction at Wootton Bassett. Then, over the course of the 'Cheltenham Flyer', the Bristol train was allowed 73 min for the concluding 77.3 miles from Swindon to Paddington, though of course from passing Swindon at full speed.

It will be seen at once from the tabulated details that despite several checks on each occasion, both trains were 4 to 5 min ahead of time on passing Southall, and could run easily in afterwards. Neither engine was pressed unduly up the Filton bank, and I have myself

GWR 12 noon Bristol-Paddington

| Engine no: | | | 2949 | | 2980 | |
| Engine name: | | | *Stanford Court* | | *Coeur de Lion* | |
Distance miles		**Schedule** min	**Actual** m s	**Speeds** mph	**Actual** m s	**Speeds** mph
0.0	BRISTOL	0	0 00	—	0 00	—
4.9	Filton Junction	9½	9 55	28½	10 06	28½
—			pws	20	—	—
7.8	Winterbourne		14 02	52	13 54	56
13.0	Chipping Sodbury		19 55	58½	19 16	61½
17.6	Badminton	25	24 46	56½	23 49	57½
23.4	Hullavington		29 42	79	28 43	80½
27.9	Little Somerford		32 59	84	31 59	85
30.6	Brinkworth		35 03	76½	34 02	78
34.7	Wootton Bassett	41	39 01	38½*	37 47	51½*
40.3	SWINDON	47	45 58	55½	43 31	64½
46.1	Shrivenham		51 36	66	48 30	74
51.1	Uffington		56 04	70	52 35	76½
53.7	Challow		—	—	54 38	77½
57.2	Wantage Road		61 09	75	57 22	79
61.1	Steventon		64 17	73	60 19	79
—			signals	—	—	—
64.5	DIDCOT	68	67 15	—	63 01	72
69.1	Cholsey		71 17	72	67 26	61
72.8	Goring		74 18	76	—	eased
76.1	Pangbourne		76 51	76½	74 59	52½
—			—	—	pws	15
79.0	Tilehurst		79 05	78	79 28	—
81.6	READING	84	81 09	78	82 43	55
86.6	Twyford		85 03	76	87 24	69
93.4	Maidenhead	94	90 28	74	92 42	81½
99.1	Slough	100	95 17	72	97 01	80
108.5	Southall	109	103 47	60	104 31	69
111.9	Ealing Broadway		signals	—	107 46	59
—						
117.6	PADDINGTON	120	118 23	—	116 07	—

*Speed restriction

recorded a higher speed at the summit of 31½ mph with *Dorney Court* on the same train; but some very fast running followed from Badminton on both the tabulated journeys, while on the second, with the engine *Coeur de Lion*, the high speed was continued from Swindon in order to have plenty in hand for the anticipated permanent way check before Reading. By that time, *Stanford Court* was nearly 3 min early, and continuing in the high 'seventies' had plenty of time in hand to offset the concluding checks. Because of the severe permanent way checks, *Coeur de Lion* was nearly 2½ min behind the other engine at Twyford, but the driver then put on a tremendous burst of speed, all on virtually level track, and for 20 miles the average was 77.5 mph with a sustained maximum of 81½

mph, and the engine was drastically eased after Southall. My own run, with *Dorney Court*, was unchecked as far as Slough, by which time we were 4 min early. The concluding delays, on a summer Saturday, were not severe and we arrived in 117½ min from Bristol, or 113 min net. The highest speeds were 79 mph at Little Somerford and 75 at Wantage Road.

The Cornish road provides a complete contrast and on a run I enjoyed in the early autumn of 1924 *Lady of Shalott* did well with a seven-coach train on the up Cornish Riviera Express, all of the heaviest 70 ft stock. I was not familiar with the gradients of that route, and took no details of maximum and minimum speeds other than the minimum in climbing the severe bank between Bodmin

GWR 3.55 pm Paddington-Newport

Run no:			1		2		3		4	
Engine no:			2916		2943		2942		2986	
Engine name:			Saint Benedict		Hampton Court		Fawley Court		Robin Hood	
Load (tons E/F):			290/310		290/310		323/340		333/360	
Distance		Schedule	Actual	Speeds	Actual	Speeds	Actual	Speeds	Actual	Speeds
miles		min	m s	mph	m s	mph	m s	mph	m s	mph
0.0	PADDINGTON	0	0 00	—	0 00	—	0 00	—	0 00	—
5.7	Ealing Broadway		8 35	—	8 25	—	8 35	—	9 00	—
—			pws	—	—	—	pws	—	—	—
9.1	Southall	11	14 05	—	11 35	67	12 30	—	12 25	61
18.5	Slough	20	23 05	71½	19 35	75	21 45	68	20 45	74
31.0	Twyford	31½	34 30	65	30 35	70	33 55	61½	31 45	66
—			—	—	signals	—	—	—	signals	—
36.0	READING	37	39 00	—	35 20	55	38 45	—	40 20	—
41.5	Pangbourne		44 00	70	41 00	—	43 55	—	47 35	—
48.5	Cholsey		50 35	—	47 35	48	50 20	67	54 25	60
53.1	DIDCOT	53	55 00	65	51 50	—	54 40	65	59 00	—
60.4	Wantage Road		61 45	—	59 00	63	61 30	65	66 00	—
—			signals	—	—	—	—	—	—	—
66.5	Uffington		70 15	—	65 00	60	67 20	65	71 40	65
71.5	Shrivenham		75 00	70	69 55	—	72 10	—	76 10	67
—			pws	—	—	—	pws	—	—	—
77.3	SWINDON	77	83 35	—	75 35	—	80 35	—	81 20	70
—			—	—	—	—	—	—	signals	—
82.9	Wootton Bassett	83	89 00	69	81 05	—	86 25	—	88 20	—
89.7	Little Somerford		95 25	72½	87 40	67	92 45	72½	94 55	67
—			—	55½*	—	57½*	—	—	—	53½
100.0	BADMINTON	103	106 10	—	99 20	—	103 30	52½	106 55	—
—			106 50	—	100 20	—	—	—	108 00	—
104.6	Chipping Sodbury		112 45	—	106 35	—	108 00	—	114 40	—
111.5	*Stoke Gifford East*	114	118 30	76½	112 55	70	114 20	69	121 05	70
—			—	—	—	—	signals	10	—	—
116.7	Pilning		123 50	—	118 20	—	121 20	—	126 45	—
—			—	—	signals	—	—	—	signals	—
123.6	Severn Tunnel Junction									
	Junction	128½	132 40	31½	129 15	—	130 00	29	136 00	—
—			signals	—	signals	—	signals	—	signals	—
133.4	NEWPORT	140	147 45	—	142 15	—	144 30	—	150 15	—

*Minimum speed on 1 in 300 before shutting off steam.

Road and Doublebois. Here the gradients change constantly, varying between 1 in 65 and 1 in 90, with much curvature, and the lowest speed was 27½ mph. From the tabulated log it will be seen that we were steadily gaining time, and passed Liskeard 3 min early. The subsequent descent to the river side approaching Saltash was taken at very moderate speed, as will be noted from the average speeds, and we arrived in Plymouth rather more than a minute early.

GWR Truro-Plymouth (North Road): The Cornish Riviera Express

Load: 7 cars, 255 tons tare, 275 tons full. Engine: No 2910 *Lady of Shalott*.

Distance miles		Schedule min	Actual m s	Average speed mph
0.0	TRURO	0	0 00	—
4.9	Probus		8 55	—
7.5	Grampound Road		12 55	39.0
12.0	Burngullow		19 35	40.5
14.3	ST AUSTELL		22 55	41.4
18.9	PAR	29	28 30	49.5
23.0	Lostwithiel		34 55	38.4
26.6	Bodmin Road	40	39 25	48.0
32.5	Doublebois	52	50 05	*33.2
36.0	LISKEARD	57	54 05	52.5
39.3	Menheniot		58 20	46.6
45.0	St Germans		65 45	46.1
49.3	Defiance platform		70 55	49.9
54.7	PLYMOUTH	81	79 20	—

*Minimum speed on bank 27½ mph

Turning now to the South Wales service, there are first of all four runs on the 3.55 pm down from Paddington, which was booked to pass Stoke Gifford East box (near the present Parkway station) in 114 min, inclusive of a conditional stop at Badminton. This was one of the trains on which the Duke of Beaufort could request a stop for himself, his family or for one of his visitors at Badminton House. The stop was made on three out of the four runs tabulated. They show clearly the ability of the 'Saint' Class engines to accelerate rapidly from rest, and from the various checks. In fact, the starts out of Paddington were a good deal faster than those usually clocked with the 'Star' Class four-cylinder engines at that time. Note should be taken also of the excellent sustained speeds on the gradual rise from Didcot to Swindon, especially that by the engine *Robin Hood*, in column four of the table. No time was wasted by the distinguished passengers detraining at Badminton, and it will be seen that in one case

the train was under way again in no more than 40 sec! No detail has been shown of the concluding stages of the journey from Stoke Gifford, where the running was so frequently checked by the congestion of the traffic through the Severn Tunnel. On one occasion only was a clear run through obtained, and then the engine *Saint Benedict* climbed the 1 in 90 gradient out of the tunnel without falling below 31½ mph.

The table on page 89 sets out details of runs on the 8.55 am and 7.55 pm expresses from Paddington, the latter being the Fishguard boat express. Both include a stop at Reading but at that time also it carried a slip portion for Bristol, which was detached at Stoke Gifford. The former provided an excellent morning service to Bristol, before the days of the high-speed 'Bristolian', when the only alternative was the lethargic 9.15 am from Paddington, via Bath. The evening slip coach service was actually advertised in Bradshaw as a 'London to Bristol, Weston-super-Mare and Taunton Express', its only disadvantage at that time in the evening was that there was no access to the restaurant car included in the main part of the train.

On the opening run to Reading, *Cefntilla Court* led off with a vigorous start, but I have seen her times from Southall to Twyford handsomely beaten by a run of my own with *Tockenham Court* on the same train with a heavier load of 365 tons. On this latter, a signal check at Old Oak Common caused us to lose about ½ min to Southall, but from there we averaged 67.3 mph to Twyford. We were badly checked outside Reading, but the net time was not more than 37½ min. I was not travelling beyond Reading on that day, neither, unfortunately, was I on another occasion when engine No 2929 *Saint Stephen* had a heavy load of 445 tons. We had begun well, but the engine was eased up a little too much after Ealing and we had not exceeded 62½ mph by Slough. Then, however, the driver must have realised he was losing time, for the effort was substantially stepped up. Speed rose to a sustained 67 mph on the slight rise beyond Maidenhead, and with a smart and undelayed finish we clocked into Reading exactly on the 40 min booked.

Of the tabulated runs, *Cefntilla Court* made a good start out of Reading, and excellent going up the moderate gradients through the Vale of the White Horse. Even better was promised after the train had passed on to the South Wales Direct line, at Wootton Bassett,

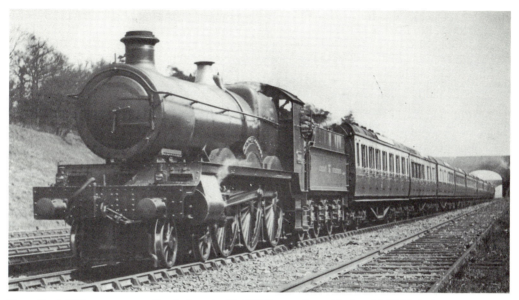

Down South Wales express near Twyford: engine No 2941 Easton Court *(the late M.W. Earley).*

for speed had been worked up to 74 mph when adverse signals compelled a dead stand at Little Somerford, at the foot of the long 1 in 300 rise to Badminton. But here speed was splendidly regained to no less than 57½ mph. Time was lost, however, by having to stop at Stoke Gifford to detach the Bristol portion instead of slipping it, at speed.

On the second of the tabulated runs, *Lady of Quality* did similar work from the start, though with a heavier train, but lost about 3 min by the signal checks at Swindon. Once on to the Badminton line, however, some splendid running was made, and with high speed afterwards (79 mph before Stoke Gifford) and for once a clear road through the tunnel, Severn Tunnel Junction was passed nearly 2 min inside schedule. There was a suggestion that on the third run *Tockenham Court*, with 435 tons, was overloaded, though as always on the steam railways of Britain one had to take into account the temperament of the driver and fireman. For if *Tockenham Court* was overloaded, how could one regard the magnificent performance of *Fawley Court* in the last column of the table?

For a closer assessment of the performance on these down South Wales expresses I have worked out the equivalent drawbar horse-power relating to some of the more notable feats of haulage and have presented them alongside in the accompanying table. The

individual efforts chosen are only those in which speed was maintained at a steady minimum figure on a rising gradient, or had been attained by acceleration against such a gradient. From the tabulated details it is evident that an exceptional effort was being made on No 2942 *Fawley Court*, with the 7.55 pm Fishguard boat express. During the classic dynamometer car trials of the new four-cylinder 4-6-0 engine No 4074 *Caldicot Castle* in 1924, on which a load of 485 tons was conveyed on three successive days, the sustained speeds up the 1 in 300 incline to Badminton were consistently at 50 to 51 mph. She was probably being steamed at the limit of which the boiler was capable, or perhaps a little beyond it, at the expense of a slightly falling water level in the boiler.

The up journeys of which four fine examples are tabulated, were all on the 10.35 am non-stop express from Newport. It was a train that originated at Carmarthen, and it was worked throughout from Swansea to Paddington by 'Saint' Class engines based at Landore. It is interesting that this train, like others on the South Wales line, was subject to no acceleration during the Inter-War period, and retained the timing of 150 min for the 133.4 miles from Newport to Paddington until the autumn of 1939.

Great Western men always said that London-South Wales was the most profit-

GWR 8.55 am and 7.55 pm Paddington-Newport

Run no:			1		2		3		4	
Engine no:			2936		2908		2954		2942	
Engine name:			Cefntilla Court		Lady of Quality		Tockenham Court		Fawley Court	
Load (tons/E/F) (a)			321/345		361/380		415/435		459/485	
(b)			263/285		300/315		354/370		335/355	
Distance miles		**Schedule min**	**Actual m s**	**Speeds mph**	**Actual m s**	**Speeds mph**	**Actual m s**	**Speeds mph**	**Actual m s**	**Speeds mph**
0.0	PADDINGTON	0	0 00	—	0 00	—	0 00	—	0 00	—
5.7	Ealing Broadway		8 15	—	9 10	—	9 40	—	10 05	—
—		—	—	—	pws	—	pws	—	—	—
9.1	Southall	12	11 45	—	14 55	—	15 25	—	13 45	—
18.5	Slough	21	20 35	69	24 25	67	25 50	62½	23 10	65
31.0	Twyford	34	32 10	65	36 30	—	38 05	—	35 15	64
36.0	READING	40	38 30	—	42 20	—	43 35	—	40 50	—
5.5	Pangbourne		8 35	—	7 55	—	8 35	—	8 10	—
12.5	Cholsey		15 30	—	15 00	—	15 30	—	14 40	60
17.1	DIDCOT	19	20 10	—	19 45	64	20 00	64½	19 05	65
24.4	Wantage Road		27 25	66	27 00	60	27 30	—	26 10	66
30.5	Uffington		33 05	67	33 10	60	33 50	—	32 05	61½
—			—	69	signals	—	pws	—	pws	—
41.3	SWINDON	43½	43 05	65	44 40	—	49 35	—	44 35	64
46.9	Wootton Bassett	49½	48 15	—	51 00	—	56 00	—	50 10	—
53.7	Little Somerford		56 05	signals	57 40	70½	62 45	67	56 40	64
—			57 30	stop	—	—	—	—	—	—
64.0	BADMINTON	67½	70 40	57½	68 20	57	74 15	52	67 45	55½
—			pws	—	—	—	—	—	—	—
68.6	Chipping Sodbury		76 50	70½	72 20	—	78 35	—	71 55	74
—			84 25	—	slip	—	slip	—	79 20	—
75.5	Stoke Gifford East	78	85 45	—	78 00	79	84 55	68	81 40	—
80.7	Pilning		92 50	72½	83 05	75	90 15	74	90 10	69
—			—	—	—	—	—	—	—	—
87.6	Severn Tunnel Junction	93	101 00	35½	91 15	34	98 20	33½	99 10	24
—			signals	—	signals	—	signals	—	signals	—
97.4	NEWPORT	105	115 00	—	106 20	—	111 45	—	114 00	—

Loads (a) to Stoke Gifford, (b) to Newport.

able of all their express passenger services. In the absence of competition it was obviously considered not worthwhile to increase the running expenses by accelerated timings, and although by 1939 'Castle' Class engines had taken over most of the principal duties, the timings remained the same as when reliance was placed entirely upon the 'Saints'. Yet within their power range they were ideal engines for the job.

The 10½-mile section between Severn Tunnel Junction and Patchway could not have been more awkward, with a heavy train. It began with the need to slow down for the crossovers at the junction station, and while the first part of the 1 in 100 ascent from the tunnel on the Gloucestershire side was straightforward enough, the second stage, through the wet, single-tracked Patchway Tunnel, also on 1 in 100, could be a nightmare. It was no

mean test of driving skill to cover that first 20.3 miles out of Newport in the even half-hour. If, as on the third run, there was a permanent check to 15 mph in the very depths of the Severn Tunnel there could be serious loss of time.

The first run, with the Guy Mannering, was entirely unchecked, and on the second, Lady Superior was delayed only in the final approach to Paddington. Having kept sectional time on that awkward initial length to Patchway, or slightly improved upon it, nothing very spectacular was required on the run eastwards from Badminton. The average speeds over the 94.2 miles thence to Ealing Broadway were 62.7 and 62.3 mph respectively.

It was different on the third run with engine No 2972 The Abbot. Because of that devastating check in the depths of the Severn

Horsepower estimates: down South Wales expresses

Engine no	Engine name	Load tons	Location (near)	Gradient 1 in	Speed mph	Equivalent DHP
2943	*Hampton Court*	310	Badminton	300	57½	980
2986	*Robin Hood*	360	Slough	Level	74	1065
2936	*Cefntilla Court*	345	Badminton	300	57½	1070
2986	*Robin Hood*	360	Uffington	754	67	1095
2936	*Cefntilla Court*	345	Uffington	754	69	1117
2908	*Lady of Quality*	380	Badminton	300	57	1167
2929	*Saint Stephen*	445	Twyford	1320	67	1212
2942	*Fawley Court*	485	Uffington	800	66	1397
2942	*Fawley Court*	485	Badminton	300	55½	1410

Tunnel the train was 6¾ min late in passing Badminton, and with another severe permanent way check to come near Wantage Road, the prospects might not have seemed very good. In fact, however, with a couple of rare enthusiasts on the footplate, determined to do their very best, the train was brought into Paddington nearly 3 min early! There was some splendid running on this trip, with the spirited downhill dash from Badminton, with mile after mile at 79 mph, the vigorous recovery from the Wootton Bassett slowing, and finally, after the Wantage check, an average speed of 68.8 mph for nearly 50 miles

of level road east of Didcot. A net gain of 13½ min on schedule time and an average speed of 58.7 mph throughout from Newport to Paddington puts this run very much among the highlights of 'Saint' performance.

On the fourth journey with a load of 420 tons, engine No 2928 *Saint Sebastian*, began extremely well, but due to passing Swindon 1¼ min early there was no need for any undue haste in the later part of the journey, though, nevertheless, it clocked up the fastest time of all in passing Reading.

The general impression one gains from a study of the table of runs is of supreme

Engine No 2931 Arlington Court *positioned on the stationary test plant in Swindon Works* (British Railways).

competence, and a margin of power in reserve to be brought forth when need be, as on the third run.

The Severn Tunnel was, of course, the major bogey in the working of such heavy trains, and with loads of more than 400 tons tare it was usual for a stop to be made for bank-engine assistance at Severn Tunnel Junction. Sometimes the pilot, normally a 2-6-2 tank engine, would be taken as far as Badminton, at others working through to Swindon, and it was on one such occasion that an outstanding performance was put up, on this same train. The engine this time was No 2902 *Lady of the Lake* and the times made in relation to the schedule of the 'Cheltenham Flyer' of the 1920s have prompted me to set them alongside some other 'Saint' performances over the same route.

The first of these runs, on the 'Flyer' itself, was the one logged in the first weeks of its operation in 1923 that sent Cecil J. Allen into such raptures of enthusiasm, but the second, equally good, was especially interesting in

showing the work of the first Churchward 4-6-0 to have the standard arrangement of piston valves and link motion providing long valve travel. Since its construction in 1903 as No 98 it had been fitted with the standard taper boiler and Swindon superheater but the machinery dated back to 1903. As will be seen from the table, No 2998 was running 4 min early, on passing Twyford.

The third run was on the 1.10 pm up from Swindon, allowed 80 min for the run, but with a late start and an enterprising crew ran up to 'Cheltenham Flyer' standard of speed with a considerably heavier load. This run was all the more creditable for being made in 1926 during the lengthy coal strike of that summer, with a tender full of imported fuel. It rather gave the lie to the assertion sometimes made that Great Western engines would run only on the best grades of Welsh coal.

Lastly, there is the magnificent performance of the *Lady of the Lake*, with a load *double* that of the 'Cheltenham Flyer', and yet by Reading equalling the latter's timing. Whether the

GWR Newport-Paddington

Run no:			1		2		3		4	
Engine no:			2984		2901		2972		2928	
Engine name:			*Guy Mannering*		*Lady Superior*		*The Abbot*		*Saint Sebastian*	
Load (tons E/F):			348/375		355/385		365/390		390/420	
Distance		Schedule	Actual	Speeds	Actual	Speeds	Actual	Speeds	Actual	Speeds
(miles)		(min)	m s	mph	m s	mph	m s	mph	m s	mph
0.0	NEWPORT	0	0 00	—	0 00	—	0 00	—	0 00	—
9.8	Severn Tunnel Junction	12	13 15	59	13 10	—	13 00	59	13 00	59
—			—	—	—	71½	pws	16	—	66
15.3	*Severn Tunnel East*		20 15	—	19 25	—	24 35	—	19 30	—
20.3	Patchway	30	30 00	25½	29 05	23½	36 15	23	29 10	24
23.5	Winterbourne		34 55	47½	33 55	50	41 25	—	34 10	—
28.8	Chipping Sodbury		41 20	51½	40 00	56	48 00	51	40 45	52
33.4	Badminton	47	47 00	44½	45 50	eased	53 40	47½	46 15	49
43.7	Little Somerford		56 45	71	55 55	74	62 50	79	55 35	75
50.5	Wootton Bassett	63	63 35	53½	62 40	50	69 00	57	61 55	57
56.1	SWINDON	69	69 50	—	69 00	—	74 30	65	67 50	—
66.9	Uffington		80 10	64	79 10	—	83 50	74	78 20	—
—			—	—	—	—	pws	10	—	—
73.0	Wantage Road		85 45	—	84 35	70	92 20	—	83 55	—
80.3	DIDCOT	95	92 10	70	90 50	70	98 55	72	90 25	69
84.9	Cholsey		96 20	—	95 10	70	102 55	—	94 50	—
91.9	Pangbourne		102 45	—	102 05	—	109 05	66	101 35	61
97.4	READING	112	108 15	55½	107 20	60½	113 50	70	107 10	—
—			—	—	—	—	—	68	pws	—
102.4	Twyford	117	113 25	—	112 10	—	118 20	69	114 00	—
109.2	Maidenhead	124	119 25	70	118 30	66½	124 05	71½	120 20	70
115.0	Slough	130	124 45	—	124 00	—	129 00	73	125 30	71
124.3	Southall	139	133 45	61½	133 15	—	137 15	67	134 30	62
127.6	Ealing Broadway		137 05	—	136 25	—	140 15	69	137 45	—
—			—	—	signals	—	—	—	signals	—
133.4	PADDINGTON	150	144 25	—	147 05	—	147 10	—	147 05	—
Net times (min)			144½		143½		136½		142¾	

West to North express at Puxton and Worle, engine No 2913 Saint Andrew (F.J. Arthur).

GWR Swindon-Paddington

Run no:		**1**		**2**		**3**		**4**	
Engine no:		2915		2998		2921		2902	
Engine name:		Saint Bartholomew		Ernest Cunard		Saint Dunstan		Lady of the Lake	
Load (tons E/F):		218/235		240/255		311/330		449/485	
Distance (miles)	**Schedule (min)**	**Actual m s**	**Speeds mph**	**Actual m s**	**Speeds mph**	**Actual m s**	**Speeds mph**	**Actual m s**	**Speeds mph**
0.0 SWINDON	0	0 00	—	0 00	—	0 00	—	0 00	—
5.7 Shrivenham		7 20	74	7 27	—	8 20	61½	8 25	61
10.7 Uffington		11 25	77½	11 47	76½	13 00	68	13 15	66
13.4 Challow		13 35	75	13 55	74	15 20	70½	15 40	68
16.9 Wantage Road		16 20	77½	16 41	77½	18 15	72½	18 45	69
—		pws	40	—	—	—	—	—	72
20.8 Steventon	20½	21 20	60	19 45	72½	21 30	—	—	—
24.2 DIDCOT	24	24 20	70½	22 23	77½	24 20	74	25 00	72
28.8 Cholsey		28 25	67	26 14	—	28 30	—	28 55	73
32.6 Goring		31 40	70½	29 28	68	31 55	—	32 05	—
35.8 Pangbourne		34 25	72½	32 17	70½	35 00	64	34 55	68
38.7 Tilehurst		36 50	76½	34 43	69	37 40	—	37 25	70
41.3 READING	40	39 00	72½	36 53	74	40 05	67	39 45	62½
46.3 Twyford	45	43 10	76½	41 05	68	44 35	65	44 30	—
—		—	—	signals	60	—	—	—	—
53.1 Maidenhead	50½	48 40	79	46 43	—	50 40	—	50 50	67
—		pws	40	—	—	—	—	—	—
58.8 Slough	55½	53 15	—	51 53	72½	55 45	70½	56 10	—
68.2 Southall	64	63 15	65	59 59	69	64 15	65	65 25	60½
71.6 Ealing Broadway		66 25	—	62 48	—	67 20	—	68 45	65
—		—	—	signals	—	—	—	—	—
77.3 PADDINGTON	75	73 35	—	70 40	—	74 15	—	76 00	—
Net times (min)		70		68¼		74¼		76*	

*Schedule 81 min from passing Swindon at full speed.

engine was running a little short of steam after this tremendous initial effort one is not to know, but in any case there was a marked easing up. Apart from that, however, the attained maximum speed of 73 mph on level track indicates a drawbar horsepower of about 1400, equal to the maximum efforts of *Fawley Court* on the 7.55 pm down from Paddington referred to earlier.

The gentleman who logged the series of runs on the 10.35 am express from Newport to Paddington was a locomotive engineer of wide experience in the recording of engine performance, from the footplate and from the dynamometer car, as well as from the ordinary carriage, as was the case in all these South Wales runs, and when submitting the details to Cecil J. Allen for use in *The Railway Magazine*, he wrote: 'The Saints, which had worked right through from Swansea, were obviously being worked almost at their limit for hours on end, and the marvel is that the engines stand such apparently merciless driving without ill effect.' The fact that this engineer's earlier professional experience had been in the locomotive department of the Midland Railway may account for his concern at the idea of engines being worked really hard.

His consternation apparently reached its climax when returning to London after the Christmas holidays of 1928. He found the 10.35 am up from Newport loaded to no less than *17* coaches, 479 tons tare, packed with passengers, and 520 tons full. The engine, *Fawley Court* once again, was given a pilot from Severn Tunnel Junction to Badminton, but from there the 100 miles to Paddington were covered in exactly 105 min. The principal passing times were:

Distance		Actual time	Average speed
miles		m s	mph
0.0	Badminton	0 00	—
5.8	Hullavington	9 30	—
22.7	Swindon	27 30	56.4
46.9	Didcot	50 15	63.9
64.0	Reading	66 10	64.0
95.8	Acton	97 30	61.3
—		pws	—
100.0	Paddington	105 00	—

This engineer concluded his letter to Allen: 'Why on earth a tired old 'Saint' to haul 520 tons on such a booking as this?' Actually the maximum effort put forth on this run did not exceed about 1100 drawbar horsepower, considerably less than some of those already described in this chapter.

This account of some of the wonderful performances put up by the 'Saint' Class engines in the 1920s may well be concluded by an example from my own personal collection. Although not involving so long sustained an effort as on some of the runs previously detailed, it showed once again the remarkable outputs of power that these engines could put forth.

Plymouth and Torquay to Birmingham and Wolverhampton express on the Teignmouth Sea Wall, in 1925, hauled by engine No 2975 Sir Ernest Palmer.

On the Thursday before Easter, 1929, I was bound for Shrewsbury and found the 2.10 pm express from Paddington running in two portions, and with the relief section a substantial train of nine coaches, headed by the *Lady of Lynn*, I took it, rather than the heavier main train, which had a 'Star'. The 2.10 pm was one of the few 2-hour Birmingham expresses that were then actually non-stop, and its booked point-to-point times made very uneven demands upon locomotive power if they were to be strictly observed. For example, the initial stage of 26.5 miles from Paddington to High Wycombe was allowed only 30 min, while subsequent sections were more easily timed.

Lady of Lynn was working through to Shrewsbury on this first part of the train, and her driver chose to maintain point-to-point times very closely, where he was not improving upon them. Actually, no 'Castle' or 'King' has improved upon the times we made that day, as far as High Wycombe, thus:

First part 2.10 pm ex-Paddington

Load: 9 cars, 295 tons tare, 320 tons full. Engine: No 2906 *Lady of Lynn*

Distance miles		Schedule min	Actual m s	Speeds mph
0.0	Paddington	0	0 00	—
3.3	Old Oak West			
	Junction	6	6 05	—
4.6	Park Royal		7 50	—
7.8	Greenford	11	11 15	62½
10.3	Northolt Junction	13½	13 40	62½
12.1	Ruislip		15 20	68
14.8	Denham		17 40	72½
17.4	Gerrards Cross		20 00	63½
21.7	Beaconsfield		24 00	64½
24.1	*Tylers Green box*		26 05	74
26.5	High Wycombe	30 (pass)	28 35	40 (slack)

Now believe it or not, the gradients from the 7th milepost out of Paddington are almost continuously adverse to Beaconsfield, and the average inclination between Mileposts 7 and 21 is 1 in 340. Our average speed here was 66 mph, but it was on the Gerrards Cross bank that the effort was so substantially stepped up. Just before Denham on a brief length of level track we reached the maximum of 72½ mph, rushed the two miles of 1 in 175 without falling below 63½ mph and then on the 1 in 254 stretch to Beaconsfield speed slightly increased to 64½ mph. It was at this stage that the equivalent drawbar horsepower reached the notable peak of 1400, showing confirmation once again of the ability of these engines to attain very high outputs of power. After this stirring initial effort, the subsequent running, in keeping strict point to point times, became a mere 'doddle', and after Banbury, delayed by holiday traffic, we were 10 min late in arriving in Birmingham.

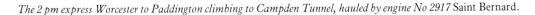

The 2 pm express Worcester to Paddington climbing to Campden Tunnel, hauled by engine No 2917 Saint Bernard.

Chapter 10

Progeny of the 'Saints'

In 1925, engine No 2925, *Saint Martin* was rebuilt with 6 ft instead of 6 ft 8½ in coupled wheels. The rebuild was quite an extensive one because the cylinders were lowered 4¼ in to maintain their position in relation to the driving wheel centres on the motion. That the engine was intended as a prototype for a new class of mixed traffic engine was generally understood at the time, in fact it was believed that a further nine engines of the 'Saint' Class were to be similarly rebuilt. But the *Saint Martin* remained an isolated engine for three years, during which time the performance was being carefully watched.

Among those with some knowledge of the inner history of the Locomotive Department of the GWR, some slight surprise was expressed that in the rebuilding of *Saint Martin* the coupled wheels should have been made 6 ft, which was a new size so far as Swindon was concerned, and in this respect it differed from

Churchward's own proposed mixed-traffic 4-6-0 of 1901, which was to have had 5 ft 8½ in coupled wheels. But this latter was to have been primarily a passenger engine for the West Country, to take over the working west of Newton Abbot, as the 'Duke' Class 4-4-0s did from the Dean 7 ft 8 in 4-2-2s, and the 'Bulldog' 4-4-0s did at a later date.

Collett's rebuild of the *Saint Martin* was to provide a mixed traffic engine of greater versatility, which would take over passenger duties on some of the steeply graded cross-country lines, as well as on the main line in Cornwall, but which would also be available for the increasing number of express freight trains, vacuum fitted throughout, that were being introduced in the later 1900s. The *Saint Martin* was accepted as an experimental prototype, but when, in 1928, the 'Hall' Class proper was introduced, there was some surprise outside the GWR, and perhaps a

Paddington-Wolverhampton express, via Oxford, on Hatton bank: engine No 4938 Liddington Hall (R. Blenkinsop).

faint touch of cynicism that so 'old fashioned' a design as that of the 'Saints' should be perpetuated in what was obviously a forward-looking modern motive power unit.

Apart from the limited use by the Southern Railway of the 4-6-0 type, with 6 ft diameter coupled wheels stemming from R.W. Urie's introduction of it in his 'H15' class on the London and South Western Railway, in 1913, the 'Hall' Class was the first large-scale use of the type as a genuine mixed traffic engine. While no one questioned the efficiency of the Great Western type of boiler, to some, the retention of the Stephenson link motion inside, seemed to suggest that in locomotive design practice Swindon was falling behind the times. Were the magnificent traditions set up by Churchward being carried forward into an age that demanded a more modern approach?

Collett was not an engine designer. That role devolved upon F.W. Hawksworth, who by that time was Chief Draughtsman. But the GWR had in the two-cylinder engine layout, applied to all the new Swindon designs except for the 'Stars', 'Castles' and 'Kings', a standard arrangement of valves and valve gear with which everyone concerned, in the running shed and in the main works, was thoroughly familiar. It may have been inaccessible by the standards of other railways, both at home and abroad, but the methods of dealing with it had become so systematised that locomotive running expenses on the Great Western were lower than those of any other British company—so why change?

Collett had experienced enough trouble with the new design of leading bogie on the 'Kings', and the changes made from the 'Court' series of 'Saints' to the 'Halls' were unconnected with the basic locomotive, but purely superficial items like the design of the cab and a more convenient positioning of the reversing gear. The boiler and front-end were identical, and the use of 6 ft diameter coupled wheels increased the nominal tractive effort from the 24,395 lb of the 'Saints' to 27,275 lb. In only one other respect did the 'Hall' Class of 1928 look different from the 'Saints', or indeed from the rebuilt *Saint Martin*, and that was in the use of a straight outside steampipe from the smoke box to the valve chest. This feature was later added to most of the 'Saints' themselves in their later years.

The first order was for no less than 80 engines of the 'Hall' Class, and 71 of them were in traffic by the end of 1929. The rest were completed early in 1930, in time to leave the works clear to proceed with the 6020-6029 batch of 'Kings'. The Great Western was then thoroughly embarked upon a fairly ruthless 'scrap and build' policy replacing old engines. The 6 ft 8½ in 4-4-0s were the principal victims at that time, and in the early 1930s the outside cylindered 'County' Class 4-4-0s were also scrapped.

In 1931, when three of the 'Saints' were withdrawn, it might have seemed that these were to go the same way. After all, the oldest of them were then nearly 30 years old and many of them had a record of very hard work behind them. As it turned out, however, although there was a strong programme of new engine building both of the 'Castle' and 'Hall' Classes throughout the 1930s, the withdrawal of the older engines was governed by the condition of individual units, mainly due to cracked frames, rather than a general policy of replacement on account of age. While it is true that none of the 'Court' series was withdrawn until after the Second World War some of the last survivors of the 'Saints' in the 1950s were some that had been built more than 45 years earlier!

For the record, the first patch of withdrawals were:

Year	No	Name
1931	2909	*Lady of Provence*
	2910	*Lady of Shalott*
	2985	*Peveril of the Peak*
1932	2900	*William Dean*
	2904	*Lady Godiva*
	2919	*Saint Cuthbert*
	2986	*Robin Hood*
1933	2901	*Lady Superior*
	2907	*Lady Disdain*
	2973	*Robbins Bolitho*
	2974	*Lord Barrymore*
	2984	*Guy Mannering*
	2998	*Ernest Cunard*
1934	2917	*Saint Bernard*
	2923	*Saint George*
	2976	*Winterstoke*
	2982	*Lalla Rookh*

It will be noted that several engines which have featured prominently in this book, by reason of excellent performance, were among the earliest victims, though as will be shown in the final chapter, some of the last to survive were among the most distinguished from the viewpoint of high power output, and high speed.

Above *Up Cornish Riviera express, ready to start from Penzance, with engine No 5915* Trentham Hall (O.S. Nock).

Below *10.30 am (Saturdays) Torquay to Paddington express near Charlton Mackrell. Engine No 5915* Trentham Hall (K.H. Leech).

Engine No 4933 Himley Hall *at Chippenham* (K.H. Leech).

The role of the 'Saint' Class, in the history of the Locomotive Department of the Great Western Railway was by no means finished when the withdrawal of some of the earlier units began in 1931. Despite the deep industrial depression that prevailed at the time, the spirit of acceleration was in the air, but with maximum economy in fuel consumption constantly in view. The testing section of the locomotive drawing office at Swindon was instructed to examine existing train schedules with a view to improvement on both the West of England and the Wolverhampton routes, from Paddington. Point-to-point timings had remained virtually unchanged since the opening of these shorter main lines, in 1906 and 1910 respectively, and both, if strictly observed, made very uneven demands upon locomotive power. The schedules on both routes had been prepared to provide easier running over the newly constructed sections, while the road was consolidating, namely from Castle Cary to Cogload Junction, and from Ashendon to Aynho Junction on both of which there were many slight, if no more than temporary restrictions. Before long both became very fast

sections, though the original point-to-point times remained unchanged.

When the question of accelerated running was investigated it was generally accepted in the drawing office at Swindon that the most economic performance of steam locomotives was obtained when the steaming rate in the boiler was kept approximately constant throughout the run. A number of tests were made, admittedly of no more than an approximate nature, to compare the fuel consumption in such ideal conditions with what was occurring in ordinary service; but the project was inhibited by the impossibility of getting confirmatory results on the stationary testing plant in Swindon works, which was not capable of absorbing more than about 500 horsepower.

It was just at this time that the campaign of Sir Nigel Gresley of the LNER, for a modern national testing plant for the British railways was gathering momentum. He enlisted the support of W.A. Stanier, who in 1932 had left the Great Western to become Chief Mechanical Engineer of the LMS, and who knew as well as anyone of the limitations of the old Churchward testing plant. Anyway

Gresley and Stanier got together, and the case for a modern British plant was underlined when Gresley felt it necessary to send his 2-8-2 express engine the *Cock O' the North* to the Vitry plant, in France, because there was nothing available in England. In the meantime the grapevine of Swindon was working overtime. By some means that was not vouchsafed, Collett became aware that a joint approach to him was being prepared for tripartite participation in the construction of a new British testing plant, with appropriate sharing of the costs, and in equal secrecy he obtained authority for modernisation of the Swindon plant to make it capable of absorbing the maximum output of the largest express locomotives.

The approach from the LNER and the LMS was duly made, and representatives of Sir Nigel Gresley and Stanier most courteously invited to Swindon for discussions. When they arrived they were conducted to the test plant, and there, to their astonishment, they saw engine No 2931 *Arlington Court* blazing away, 'flat-out', and developing something like 1200 indicated horsepower. The air compressor plant for absorbing power had been discarded, and the new control system had been applied to the friction brake wheels. Furthermore, it was explained to the visitors that while the 'Saint' was by no means the most powerful of Great Western express passenger locomotives, the control system now applied to the brake wheels was capable of absorbing at least 2000 indicated horsepower, and a good deal more, if need be.

In other words, there was no need for the Great Western Railway to join forces with the LNER and the LMS in building a new testing station. The existing one could accommodate the largest 'Pacific' engines, if need be. So Gresley and Stanier had to go it alone, because with the rather 'prickly' personality of Collett any question of testing non-Great Western engines at Swindon would have been fraught with problems!

In the meantime, while the 'Saints' themselves were declining in numbers, if not necessarily in potentiality, their progeny in the form of the 'Hall' Class were multiplying exceedingly. By the autumn of 1936 there were 165 of them at work, and the completion of engine No 5965, *Woollas Hall*, was followed immediately at Swindon by the production of the first of what could be called another off-

12 noon Bristol to Paddington express, leaving Middle Hill Tunnel, engine No 7904 Fountains Hall *(K.H. Leech).*

spring of the 'Saints', the 5 ft 8½ in 4-6-0 of the 'Grange' Class. Nevertheless, although this new class, which eventually numbered 80, would appear to have been exactly in accord with Churchward's original proposals of 1901, the 'Granges' were actually replacements of the '4300' and '5300' Classes of 2-6-0, which had 5 ft 8½ in wheels and which were being scrapped at that time. The 'Granges', like the 'Halls' had exactly the same boiler as the 'Saints', and because of the smaller coupled wheels had a nominal tractive effort of 28,800 lb.

The 'Saints' might be getting old, but they could still put up some magnificent performances when necessary. In the mid-1930s, No 2937 *Clevedon Court*, which used to be at Exeter, and was a visitor to Penzance on the West of England Postal from time to time, was standing pilot at Reading, and in 1936, within a relatively short space of time, she was called upon for top class express duty at a moment's notice on no less than three recorded occasions.

The first instance took place on April 7, when the 3.30 pm West of England express from Paddington was observed arriving at Plymouth (North Road) only about 5 min behind *Clevedon Court*. This train had stops at Taunton, Exeter, and Newton Abbot, with an allowance of only 5 min over the level 3 hours from Paddington to Exeter. The initial load would be much less west of Newton Abbot by the detaching of the Torquay line portion, but it was evident that some excellent work had been done after *Clevedon Court* had been substituted for the regular engine. The next occasion came only a fortnight later, and was reported in more detail by a correspondent of *The Railway Magazine* who was travelling from Paddington to Taunton.

At the time of the centenary of the Great Western Railway the train service to the West of England was augmented by a second morning express leaving Paddington 5 min after the Cornish Riviera. The latter express carried through portions for none save Cornish destinations, while the 10.35 am served stations and routes previously covered by slip portions off the Cornish Riviera Express. The 10.35 slipped a portion for Weymouth at Heywood Road Junction, but stopped at Taunton, to detach its through carriages for Ilfracombe and Minehead, and at Newton Abbot to detach its Kingsbridge through carriage.

The Railway Magazine correspondent was first of all surprised that when approaching Reading his train was drastically slowed down, and then put through the relief line platform, before crossing over to take the Berks and Hants line and to continue normally. But while passing through Reading station he was astonished to see that the 'King' Class engine on the Cornish Riviera had coupled off, and was in the process of being replaced—yes, by *Clevedon Court*! The 'Castle' working his own train recovered the time lost by the diversion through the relief line platform at Reading, and reached Taunton at 12.57 pm on time in 142 min from Paddington (142.7 miles). Having detached the Ilfracombe and Minehead portions it left again at 1 pm. Not being in any hurry to leave the station he waited. Very soon afterwards the down main line signals were pulled off, and at 1.5 pm the 'Limited' stormed through, with *Clevedon Court* going 'flat out', as that correspondent put it.

Unfortunately, no one thought to ask the traffic department for copies of the guard's journals on what must have been two notable examples of 'Saint' performance, but *Clevedon Court*'s hour of glory was not yet finished, and on the third occasion there was fortunately a very experienced recorder travelling passenger on the train. Having come to the rescue of the 3.30 pm from Paddington, and then the 'Cornish Riviera' it was next the turn of the 'Bristolian', of all trains, then regularly worked by a 'King'.

With engine No 6015, *King Richard III* the London driver had made an exceptionally vigorous start; too vigorous perhaps, because by Maidenhead the engine was running hot, and had to be eased down. One could imagine the driver echoing the cry of the engine's namesake, 450 years earlier: 'A horse! a horse! my kingdom for a horse!' Certainly his distress signal was very promptly and efficiently answered, for when he stopped at Reading *Clevedon Court* was ready; the changing of engines took, to be precise, no more than 6 min 57 sec. The London driver and fireman took over the Reading pilot. The rare quality of the 'Saint' Class locomotives was never displayed better than on this occasion, for although a top-link Old Oak engineman would have been familiar enough with the running characteristics of these famous engines, Reading shed cannot have had much more than 5 min notice that their standing pilot was needed, and to get her ready for what was involved.

Up West of England express leaving Reading with engine No 6990 Witherslack Hall (the late M.W. Earley).

Up Torquay and Paignton express on the Bruton bank, hauled by engine No 7909 Heveningham Hall (K.H. Leech).

In earlier chapters of this book I have detailed various fast-running exploits of the 'Saint' Class engines when they were new, or sharing the top-link honours with the 'Stars', but rarely can they have been called upon for such an effort as this. The schedule of the down 'Bristolian' allowed no more than 72 min for the 82¼ miles from passing Reading at full speed to arriving at Temple Meads, an average speed of 68.5 mph, and this included the regular speed restriction to about 30 mph through Bath. No such assignment was ever given to the 'Saints' in their main line hey-day and in 1936 with what would officially have been considered a totally unsuitable engine for the job, no blame would have been laid upon the driver and fireman if they had lost time. In that halcyon year, however, the reputation of *Clevedon Court* as a substitute would probably not have been entirely unknown among the top-link Old Oak drivers, since in April that year she had twice taken over the haulage of crack West of England expresses, and worked through to Plymouth. So, on this third occasion, the driver set about the continuation of the run to Bristol as though he had a 'Star' engine—which indeed it was soon proved he had!

In presenting the accompanying log of the journey it should be explained that the meticulously accurate recorder of the times and speeds, the late R.E. Charlewood, always timed to mileposts at or near the stations, instead of using the easier but less precise method of timing to the centre of the station, and using a distance, to the first place of decimals of a mile approximating to the exact chainage quoted in the working timetable. Thus at Didcot, for example, Mr Charlewood timed to Milepost 53¼, at Wootton Bassett to Milepost 83, and so on. But his methods only serve to underline the authenticity of the outstanding performance he recorded.

At the very start there was none of the 'warming-up' that one might have expected on a locomotive requisitioned at little more than a moment's notice. They got away from Reading with electrifying vigour, and on level track were doing 78 mph in 9 min from the dead start. There were slight signal checks on either side of Steventon, which cost about 1¼ min, but then the driver took the engine into a magnificent piece of running up through the Vale of the White Horse. In studying the speeds set out in the table it should be appreciated that except for a single mile of level track, before Shrivenham, the line is rising throughout. The gradient is nowhere steeper than 1 in 660, but even on a rise of 1 in 834, about 200 horsepower is needed to overcome the force of gravity upon an engine and train totalling 340 tons at 83½ mph. The train resistance would require about 700 horsepower, thus leaving the remarkable equivalent drawbar horsepower of 900 at 83½ mph.

During the exhaustive stationary plant and dynamometer trials of one of the 'King' Class engines in 1952 the maximum equivalent drawbar horsepower at 83 mph was 1000, this with the boiler steamed up to the maximum rate that could be sustained continuously, and by comparison it might at first seem unbelievable that a 'Saint', with a considerably smaller boiler should be able to approach so closely to the 'King' maximum. It is fairly certain, however, that on *Clevedon Court* some mortgaging of boiler capacity must have taken place after Challow.

The speed was eased a little through Swindon and on the falling gradient of 1 in 660 to Wootton Bassett the speed did not at first exceed 80 mph, and the equivalent drawbar horsepower represented by this would not have been more than 400, a very big difference from the 900 between Shrivenham and Milepost 75½. Not that there was any slackening of the effort in terms of speed, and at the foot of the Dauntsey bank the thrilling maximum of 90 mph was sustained for a full mile. The signal check at Chippenham cost about a minute, and speed was restrained to no more than 76½ mph descending through the Box Tunnel, and in the outer approaches to Bath. A minute had been dropped on the sectional time of 58½ min from Reading to Bath; but the checks between them had cost 2¼ min, and net time from Didcot was only 41¼ min, against the 45 min scheduled.

The flying average over the 64½ miles from Pangbourne to Milepost 106 (covered in 51 min 56 sec) was 74.5 mph all checks included, or no less than 77.8 mph net, and on the final length where the booked point-to-point time gives a little margin for recovery, a little time was gained, despite checks from Keynsham inwards. Charlewood estimated the net time from start to stop as 69 min, but at the normal speed of the 'Bristolian' passing Reading, the 8¾ miles to Goring would have taken about 6¾ min instead of the actual 9¼ min from a dead start, so in comparison with the 'Bristolian' schedule the running of *Clevedon Court* was equivalent to a net time of 66½ min from Reading to Bristol, a remarkable gain of 5½ min on schedule, and a pass to stop average speed of 74 mph—an astonishing performance.

At a time when more and more 'Castles' were being built new at Swindon, not to mention the direct progeny, in the form of 'Halls' and 'Granges', one might justifiably have imagined that the day of the 'Saints' was all but finished, and that save for an occasional swan-song like that of *Clevedon Court* we had virtually heard the end of them by the late 1930s. Then came the Second World War and circumstances led to my using the West to North route from Bristol via the Severn Tunnel on occasions. I saw a number of them still at work, though it was not until after the war that I recorded a performance coming anywhere near one noted by my friend D.S.M. Barrie, on the wartime 12.45 pm from Cardiff. With such a load as 465 tons it was not surprising that engine No 2949 *Stanford Court* was provided with a pilot up the steep gradient from Caerleon to Pontypool Road, a 4-4-0 of the 'Bulldog' Class, the *Sir Massey Lopes*, because the allowance of no more than 15 min was an exceedingly sharp one for the distance of ten miles from Newport, including

such a bank. Indeed the two engines together took 15 min 47 sec start to stop.

With no more than a slight reduction of the load to 450 tons my friend was surprised to see the 4-4-0 detached, and, unassisted, the 'Saint' then proceeded to put up yet another of those performances that have astonished and delighted their admirers over so many years. Again, for a full appreciation of what took place one must bear in mind the gradient profile. From Pontypool Road the line falls to the crossing of the River Usk just before Penpergwn station, but one cannot take full advantage of this descent to rush the earlier part of the climb to Llanvihangel because of a speed restriction over the river bridge at the very foot of the incline. *Stanford Court* had been doing 66 mph before this, but was braked to 55 mph round the curve, and with this rather intimidating start to it the ascent to Llanvihangel was little short of phenomenal. The first three miles to Abergavenny are inclined at 1 in 154-181-153, and on passing the latter station the speed had not fallen below 43 mph. Then came the real crunch: two miles at 1 in 85-82 followed by one and three-quarter miles at 1 in 95 to the summit.

Engine No 5915 Trentham Hall *newly outshopped in the BR lined black livery at Bath* (K.H. Leech).

GWR 'The Bristolian' in 1936: Reading-Bristol (Temple Meads)

Engine: No 2937 *Clevedon Court*. Load: 7 cars, 216 tons tare, 225 tons full.

Distance* miles		Schedule min	Actual m s	Speeds mph
0	READING	0	0 00	—
5½	Pangbourne		6 32	—
8¾	Goring		9 15	78
12½	Cholsey		12 09	77½
17¼	DIDCOT	13½	15 53	76
—			signals	60
20½	Steventon	16½	18 35	—
—			signals	55
24½	Wantage Road		22 32	—
28	Challow		25 34	75
30½	Uffington		27 34	76½
35½	Shrivenham		31 21	82
39½	*Milepost 75½*		34 16	83½
41¼	SWINDON	33½	35 34	78
47	Wootton Bassett		39 57	80
51¾	Dauntsey		43 19	90
56	*Milepost 92*		46 18	83½
—			signals	—
58	CHIPPENHAM	47	48 18	46½
62¼	Corsham		52 15	72½
65	*Milepost 101*		54 28	76½
70	*Milepost 106*		58 28	—
70⅞	BATH	58½	59 29	34†
75¼	Saltford		63 55	72
77¾	Keynsham		65 55	76½
—			psw	—
80¾	St Annes Park		68 50	40
—			signals	—
82¼	BRISTOL	72	72 28	—

Net time 69 min

* to exact mileposts. † speed restriction.

Now over the years I have personally made quite a number of runs over this route mostly with 'Castle', Class engines, and some from the 'privileged observer' post of the footplate, and never even with loads considerably less than the 450 tons hauled by *Stanford Court*, have I seen this bank climbed at anything approaching such a speed. On the 1 in 85-82 section they did not fall below 29 mph and on the final 1 in 95 actually accelerated, to 31 mph. On a post-war run when riding on a 'Castle' in superb condition the corresponding speeds with a 460 ton load were 17½ and 22 mph using a fully opened regulator and 38 per cent cut-off. The equivalent drawbar horse-powers approaching Llanvihangel summit were 830 by *Clifford Castle*, and 1300 by *Stanford Court*.

The finest uphill performance I have noted at relatively low speed by a 'Castle' Class engine, several times repeated in the course of a through working from Shrewsbury to Newton Abbot, was a sustained speed of 34 mph on 1 in 100, with a load of 445 tons, representing an equivalent drawbar horse-power of 1330, but it must be added that in my experience it was exceptional. Even in this instance, however, the EDHP in relation to the nominal tractive effort of the locomotive was considerably less than that of *Stanford Court*: 94.2, against 118.2, taking the value of the tractive effort in tons, a 25 per cent advantage in favour of the 'Saint'. No more striking example could be quoted of the effectiveness of the Swindon setting of the Stephenson link motion on these two-cylinder 4-6-0 locomotives. With the end of the war the curtain was poised to rise upon the brilliant and final stage of the story.

Chapter 11

The brilliant finale

When the Great Western Railway published its first post-war edition of the famous *Engine Book*, in 1946 there were 48 of the 'Saint' Class out of the original 77 remaining in service. These included five 'Ladies', 11 'Saints', all 25 of the 'Courts' including No 2935 which had been fitted with poppet valve gear, two of the original 4-6-0s of 1905, and five that had begun life as 'Atlantics'. During the war I had been travelling to Oswestry on occasions, and had become aware of the spirited performances frequently put up on the main line between Wolverhampton and Chester; then, free of wartime restrictions, I took the opportunity of seeking out the performances of these engines. I was rewarded with some notable experiences. At the same time, increasingly close acquaintance with the route and its running led me to suspect some of the published details of its gradients, particularly between Shifnal and Wellington.

In the years between the wars, *The Railway Magazine* built up a bank of information of impeccable accuracy on such railway statistics as mileages, physical features and such like; but 'even Homer nods', and the draughtsman who drew the profile of the GWR main line north from Wolverhampton certainly did so when he got to Shifnal. In 1946 the Chief Civil Engineer kindly confirmed for me that over the 2¾ miles from Shifnal to Hollinswood summit the inclination is 1 in 100, not 1 in 150, and that the first two miles of the ensuing descent towards Wellington the gradient is 1 in 120, not 220.

One day in the summer of 1948 I was bound for Chester, and having travelled to Birmingham by the Midland route from Bath I joined the 9.10 am from Paddington at Snow Hill, a very heavy and crowded 13-coach train, hauled as usual by a 'King'. At Wolverhampton we changed engines, and in the heavy exchange of passengers I managed to get a window corner on the milepost side. I noted also that while the load remained unchanged at a massive total of 480 tons behind the tender I could see that the fresh engine was a very grimy 'Saint'. I was not able to establish its identity until we reached Chester, such was the crowding of the train and the risk of losing one's seat by vacating it even briefly. The engine proved to be No 2926, *Saint Nicholas*,

5 pm Chester to Paddington express near Wrexham: Engine No 2930 Saint Vincent. *(The author is on the footplate.)* (W.A. Camwell).

and 'Father Christmas' certainly had a treat in store for me that day. As on many of what could be called secondary, or feeder routes, train timings had remained sharp during the war years, and the allowance of 24 min, for the 19.6 miles from Wolverhampton to Wellington was the same as that worked by the 6.10 pm from Paddington when I first began to travel over this route, in 1928. As we set out on this 1948 occasion I thought back to 'Saint' runs of old, when *Lady Godiva* took out no more than 285 tons, *Stackpole Court* had 320 tons, and when a couple of '4300' Class Moguls were provided for no more than 285 tons. And here, 20 years later, was *Saint Nicholas* starting away with 480 tons!

As we got away, admittedly on falling gradients at the start, I thought of that correspondent of *The Railway Magazine*, in 1929, who deplored the use, even then, of 'tired old Saints', on heavy express trains. It was soon evident that we were going even faster than those runs of 20 years ago, reaching 75 mph down the Albrighton bank, and clearing Hollinswood bank at the remarkable minimum speed of 38½ mph. It is true speed was still falling at the summit, as one would naturally expect on a 1 in 100 gradient with a load of 480 tons, but over the last mile the drop was only 4½ mph. Moreover, we kept exactly that sharp timing of 24 min to Wellington, and then ran hard downhill to improve slightly

upon the allowance of 15 min for the 10.3 miles on to Shrewsbury, passing Upton Magna, 6.8 miles, in 8¼ min at 68½ mph. As if this were not enough, not long after I had enjoyed this run one of my Birmingham friends, a recorder of long experience, sent me details of an occasion when *Saint Bartholomew* was on the same job, and reached Wellington a clear minute *faster* than my time. The load was certainly one coach less, 445 tons behind the tender, but the speeds were splendid: 78 mph down the Albrighton bank, after a faster start than mine, and 39 mph minimum at Hollinswood.

At Shrewsbury, on my own run, the load was reduced by five coaches, leaving a total of 300 tons behind the tender, and over this sharply graded northern end of the main line the driver of *Saint Nicholas* set about things as though he were working the 'Cheltenham Flyer'! From the 'King' which had brought the train down from London he had inherited a late start of 15 min. It was not to be expected that any of this would be recovered while the load remained at 480 tons, and he left Shrewsbury with the train still 15 min late. Gobowen, the next stopping station, stands at a considerably higher level than Shrewsbury. The start is steeply adverse, and after passing Leaton, on a rise of 1 in 165, at 55 mph, the line, although sharply undulating, continues upward on the average. But *Saint Nicholas* ran

Just after the Second World War at Gobowen: engine No 2903 Lady of Lyons, *in plain green.*

at speeds fluctuating thus: 71½, 66, 77, 65, 72½, 67, 69 and finally down to 60 when steam was shut off for Gobowen, to complete the 18 miles from Shrewsbury in 20 min.

A sharp run over the next 7.4 miles to Ruabon, in 9¾ min, and we left there only 7 min late. Much more time regaining, however, could not be expected, because there was a slowing to 5 mph over a track subsidence before Wrexham, and speed was required to be severely restrained down the steep Gresford bank, owing to curvature. So the last 12.1 miles from Wrexham into Chester took 18¼ min. Even so, we were only 5 min late on arrival—a very enterprising piece of work by the crew of the *Saint Nicholas*.

One could not fail to be other than deeply impressed by performances such as the foregoing by engines that, statistically at any rate, were 40 years old. One is well enough aware that in their long life many of the working parts would have been renewed, quite apart from the boiler, but it was after all the frames, the backbone of the engine, which were the governing factors, and their longevity, despite their duplex nature with the 'bar' section at the front end, was a resounding tribute to the excellence of the original design.

I was interested to see other engines of the class, including an even greater veteran, No 2903, the *Lady of Lyons* still hard at work on the Chester road, and in that same year Mr Hawksworth, who was then still in command at Swindon, arranged for me to make some footplate journeys to see the working for myself. On the 5 pm up from Chester we had engine No 2930, *Saint Vincent*. I was sorry in a way not to have one of the more disreputable looking members of the class, for No 2930 had not long returned from Swindon and had been repainted. Actually she had not had the most complete of overhauls, but the kind referred to in the works as 'a sole and heel job'. Nevertheless, with the copper on her chimney top once more burnished, after its wartime covering up with black paint, and the safety valve bonnet once more polished she looked well, although the green paint was unlined. She had not yet acquired a smokebox numberplate (á la BR) and the tender carried no evidence of ownership.

The driver and fireman, both Chester men, were named Hughes, though no relation to each other. John, the fireman, was later transferred to Crewe and rose high in the Motive Power Department of the London Midland Region. I enjoyed many more footplate journeys in his company on diesel and 25kV electric locomotives when he was Chief Motive Power Inspector of the Region, mainly between Crewe and Carlisle.

In 1948 I found the *Saint Vincent* an excellent engine. What intrigued me especially was to find not only that the train was running to sharper timings than those I had noted on this route 20 years earlier, but to note the superiority of the engine performance at every point. We began, for example, with an excellent sustained 31 mph up the 1 in 82 of Gresford bank, which with our 300-ton train meant just over 1000 equivalent drawbar horsepower; but the greatest contrast between past and present was on leaving Gobowen, for the 18-mile sprint to Shrewsbury. In 1929, *Saint Nicholas*, with a 335-ton load, ran at 53 to 65 mph over this undulating road. In 1948, *Saint Vincent*, with 300-tons, tore over this same line at between 63 and 76½ mph.

But it was after leaving Shrewsbury, when our load had been augmented by the addition of four fully loaded milk tank wagons, weighing 28 tons each, that the comparison between past and present became so striking, and I have set out in tabular form details of our running alongside two other 'Saint' performances with comparable loads on the one-time 4.35 pm express and made some 20 years earlier. The schedule was in each case 15 min for the 10.3 miles from Shrewsbury to Wellington, but for the continuation 19.6 miles on to Wolverhampton the allowance was 28 min in 1928-9, but only 26 min in 1948. From the start, once the very sharp curve out of the station has been negotiated, the line undulates to the crossing of the River Severn a mile beyond Upton Magna station, after which the climb to Wellington is almost continuous at 1 in 185-200-120. From the table it will be seen that *Saint Vincent* left his rivals fairly standing, with a maximum of 67 mph at the river crossing and the remarkable minimum of 55 mph above Adamston. It was the same leaving Wellington on the steep ascent to Hollinswood. Once over the top the drivers on the two earlier occasions sneaked an advantage over us by turning a blind eye to the 60 mph speed restriction through Shifnal station. Both went through at an unrestrained 69 mph and so achieved a higher maximum at the foot of the bank. Our driver, with an inspector at his elbow, was more circumspect, and did not open out until we were through the station. It will be seen, however, that despite the lowest maximum *Saint Vincent*

Above *Engine No 2906* Lady of Lynn *in BR plain black.*

Below *Engine No 2950* Taplow Court, *in 1951, on Paddington–Bristol (via Devizes) express passing Enborne Junction, Newbury* (J.F. Russell-Smith).

GWR Shrewsbury-Wolverhampton

Year:		1928		1929		1948	
Engine no:		2990		2924		2930	
Engine name:		*Waverley*		*Saint Helena*		*Saint Vincent*	
Load (tons E/F):		369/410		347/375		386/415	
Distance		**Actual**	**Speeds**	**Actual**	**Speeds**	**Actual**	**Speeds**
miles		**m s**	**m s**	**m s**	**mph**	**m s**	**mph**
0.0	SHREWSBURY	0 00	—	0 00	—	0 00	—
3.8	Upton Magna	7 30	60	7 05	58½	6 07	67
8.6	Admaston	13 00	43	12 40	43	10 00	55
10.3	WELLINGTON (SALOP)	15 45	—	15 05	—	13 35	—
2.9	Oakengates	8 15	31	7 05	33½	6 25	36
4.2	*Hollinswood*	10 15	31½	9 00	33½	8 15	38
7.1	Shifnal	13 30	69	12 15	69	11 48	60*
—		—	76½	—	79	—	74½
11.8	Albrighton	17 50	—	16 25	—	16 08	—
—	*Milepost 148*	—	45	—	44¼	—	48
14.8	Codsall	21 20	64½	20 00	62½	19 27	64
—		—	—	signal check	—	signals	—
19.6	WOLVERHAMPTON	28 20	—	27 35	—	26 02	—

*Speed restriction

took the subsequent climb to Milepost 148 (3½ miles at 1 in 137-100) at a higher speed than either of the other two engines.

Then, again in 1948, Swindon had yet another and final treat in store for me with these engines. Swindon shed used to work the 10.50 am express up to Paddington, which was a combined train with portions from Bristol and Cheltenham, and at that time it usually had a 'Saint' or a 'Star', for a 12-coach train. It would not have seemed a very exciting job, having regard to what the 'Saints' were required to do in the past, with intermediate stops to make at Didcot and Reading. The engine, too, looked no 'glamour girl'. Although she had recently had a 'sole and heel' there was hardly a vestige of paint showing, though in its previous personal association with Churchward himself it was pleasant to have No 2934, *Butleigh Court*. But when we got away, with load of 410 tons, it was evident that despite her dingy appearance she was a perfect lady of a locomotive. She worked easily up to a maximum speed of 69½ mph on the slight descending gradient from Shrivenham, and went as easily and quietly up to 66 mph on the dead level between Didcot and Reading. But I was especially interested to experience how smooth her action was, even when pulled up to as short a cut-off as 20 per cent—far more so than *Saint Vincent*.

Then, we were kept standing a little more than our allotted station times at Reading, while many more passengers entrained, and with a permanent way check to 15 mph to be observed near Southall, the driver opened her up rather more on leaving Reading. As we got away, and began to develop a perfect hurricane of a stride, I thought once again of the man who talked about 'tired old Saints' in 1929! The driver used relatively short cut-offs —for these engines—but a wider regulator opening, and this is what happened, on virtually dead level track.

Distance		**Actual**	**Speeds**
miles		**m s**	**mph**
0.0	Reading	0 00	—
3.0	Milepost 33	5 42	52
5.0	Twyford	7 51	61½
8.0	Milepost 28	10 37	68
11.8	Maidenhead	13 48	74
15.0	Burnham (Bucks)	16 21	77
17.5	Slough	18 23	72½
21.25	Iver	21 33	70
25.1	Hayes	24 47	72½

After that came the slowing down for the 15 mph speed restriction. She was working in 25 per cent cut-off from Twyford, and a little inside 20 per cent from Maidenhead, and yet we were whirling this load, which had been increased to about 420 tons, at Reading, at 77 mph on a descending gradient of no more than 1 in 1320. It was thrilling indeed, especially to record such an outstanding piece of engine performance from the footplate.

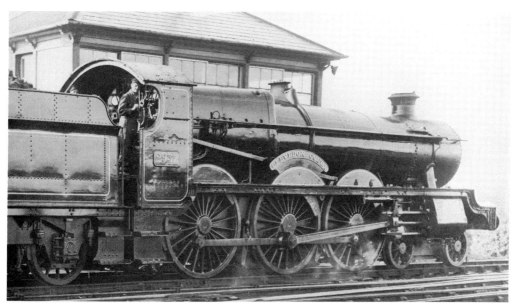

Engine No 2937 Clevedon Court *in BR lined black style* (K.H. Leech).

All that remains to be said is that after observing the speed order, the engine was worked vigorously up to 67 mph before passing Old Oak Common, and that despite the check we reached Paddington in 38½ min from Reading. Net time for the 36-mile run was exactly 36 min.

So we come to a final appraisal of these splendid engines. The memory of them remains so evergreen that at times it is difficult to recall that the last of them, the *Saint David*, went to the scrap-heap as long as 30 years ago. But it is no more remarkable that work of the quality described in this chapter, by *Saint Bartholomew, Saint Nicholas, Saint Vincent* and *Butleigh Court*, could have been done by engines with such a long history of hard work already far behind them.

To summarise these maximum efforts a table has been prepared showing ten instances. These include the two remarkable runs of 1910 and 1912, and regarding the former, with engine No 2930, *Saint Vincent*, it is quite likely, though not confirmed, that the engine was then non-superheated. The circumstances of each of these performances has been most carefully scrutinised to make sure that the speeds on rising gradients were, in fact, sustained. In certain cases, as with Nos 2949, 2930 (in 1948) 2906, and 2937 the speeds quoted were inclined to be rising. The train resistance component has been calculated using the Johansen formula established after one of the most comprehensive investigations during the inter-war years. It was later shown to give results that were somewhat on the high side for modern British Railways stock.

No modern test results were obtained with the 'Saint' Class engines using the techniques developed at Swindon by S.O. Ell, but it is interesting to compare those obtained with the 'King' Class engine No 6001, after its draughting arrangements had been modified. In studying the second table, which sets ten of the more outstanding 'Saint' performances alongside, it is important to bear in mind that those for the 'King' relate to the power output that could be sustained for an hour or more at the maximum steaming rate of which the boiler was capable, fed by two firemen. By contrast, most of the 'Saint' efforts were of short duration, when climbing a severe incline, as in the first instance tabulated, of No 2949 *Stanford Court* at Llanvihangel.

It was probable in this instance, as with certain others, that the engine was being steamed at a higher rate than the boiler could sustain indefinitely. On the other hand, the working of engine No 2943, *Hampton Court* on the Cornish Riviera Express in 1912 was part of an effort that was sustained with little variation for the first 1¼ hours of the journey, from Paddington to Savernake. Similarly in 1910, No 2930, *Saint Vincent* on the 4.15 pm

'Saint' Class: maximum performance

Year	Engine no and name	Load tons	Location	Gradient 1 in	Speed mph	Calculated equivalent drawbar horsepower
1940	2949 *Stanford Court*	450	Llanvihangel	95R	31	1300
1948	2930 *Saint Vincent*	415	Hollinswood	120R	38	1205
1928	2942 *Fawley Court*	485	Badminton	300R	55½	1410
1912	2943 *Hampton Court*	535	Kintbury	690R	60	1340
1929	2906 *Lady of Lynn*	320	Beaconsfield	254R	64½	1400
1928	2942 *Fawley Court*	485	Uffington	834R	67	1328
1910	2930 *Saint Vincent*	520	Slough	Level	70	1290
1928	2902 *Lady of the Lake*	485	Didcot	1320F	73	1230
1948	2934 *Butleigh Court*	420	Slough	Level	77	1100
1938	2937 *Clevedon Court*	225	Marston E	834R	83½	900

R = Rising gradient. F = Falling gradient

Left Ivanhoe, *withdrawn. A view of the cab taken when in the scrap-yard at Swindon* (K.H. Leech).
Below *Two 'Courts' awaiting their end at Swindon: No 2954* Tockenham Court, *and 2951* Tawstock Court (K.H. Leech).

The last survivor: engine No 2920 Saint David *outside the works administration block at Swindon* (K.H. Leech).

from Paddington sustained a remarkable level of performance for the first ¾ of an hour of the run to Bath.

A power output comparison

Speed mph	'Saint' Class Maximum estimated EDHP		'King' Class Maximum continuous steam rate (Swindon tests) Equivalent DHP
	Engine no	Equivalent DHP	
31	2949	1300	1800
38	2930	1200	1800
55½	2942	1410	1600
60	2943	1340	1520
64½	2906	1400	1420
67	2942	1395	1370
70	2930	1290	1310
73	2902	1230	1270
77	2934	1100	1140
83½	2937	900	1000
Nominal tractive effort (lb)		24,395	40,300
Maximum steam rate (lb per hour)		23,110*	33,600

*Swindon tests on 'Hall' Class 4-6-0

Related to the nominal tractive effort, these maximum 'Saint' Class performances, in comparison with those of the 'King' seem to border on the phenomenal, and make one regret that full thermodynamic trials were not conducted with one of these engines to establish just what it was in their design and working details that enabled such work to be performed. The stationary plant and road trials with one of the latest 'Hall' Class engines just after nationalisation did not give a clue, for at the maximum steam rate the equivalent drawbar horsepower at 70 mph was no more than 870. One can hardly suggest that the 1910 performance of engine No 2930 was a transitory effort, seeing that it was the peak speed of a spell of 28¾ min duration in which the average speed over a faintly rising road was 67 mph. The train, of 16 vehicles, included a mixture of elliptical- and clerestory-roofed coaches, which in the aggregate would have a higher average train resistance than that given by the Johansen formula of the 1930s. The equivalent drawbar horsepower of about 1300 on an average rising gradient of 1 in 2900 would have been sustained continuously for about half an hour —hardly a transitory effort.

Appendix

'Saint' Class 4-6-0s—leading dimensions

Boiler:
    Pressure   **225 lb per sq in**
    Tubes, small:
        Number   **176**
        Outside diameter   **2 in**
    Superheater flues:
        Number   **14**
        Outside diameter   **$5\frac{1}{8}$ in**
    Length between tube plates   **15 ft 2 in**

Heating surface: **sq ft**
    Small tubes   **1,402.5**
    Superheater flues   **284.1**
    Firebox   **154.8**
    Superheater elements   **262.6**
    Total   **2,104**

Grate area   **27.07 sq ft**

Cylinders:
    Diameter   **$18\frac{1}{2}$ in**
    Stroke   **30 in**

Motion:
    Type   **Stephenson**
    Piston valve diameter   **10 in**
    Maximum valve travel   **$6\frac{1}{4}$ in**
    Steam lap   **$1\frac{5}{8}$ in**
    Exhaust clearance   **Nil**
    Lead in full fore gear   **0.15 in**
    Cut off in full gear   **77.5 per cent**

Tractive effort at 85 per cent working
    pressure   **24,395 lb**

Weight, in working order:
    Engine only   **72 tons**
    Max axle load   **18.4 tons**
    Tender (6 tons coal 3,500 gal water) **40 tons**

118

Index

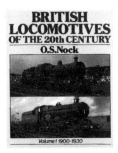

The best in railway reading

British Locomotives of the 20th Century
Vol 1: 1900-1930
O.S. Nock
The first volume of three describing and illustrating in depth the development, design and mechanical features of all British locomotive types from 1900 to the present day. Containing plans, diagrams and photographs, as well as details of service and anecdotes about the people intimately concerned with British locomotive development, this definitive work will stand as a permanent tribute to the imagination and skill of British engineers.
(*Vol 2: 1930-1960* and *Vol 3: 1960-Present Day* in preparation.)

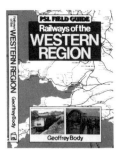

PSL Field Guide
Railways of the Western Region
Geoffrey Body
The first of five gazetteers to the sites and sights of railway significance, historical and modern, within the boundaries of the modern British Rail Regions. Ideal for use on a train journey, enabling details of a route to be followed, for touring in a car or for general reference. Contains many maps and photographs.
(*Railways of the Southern Region* in preparation.)

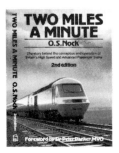

Two Miles a Minute
The story behind the conception and operation of Britain's High Speed and Advanced Passenger Trains
2nd edition
O.S. Nock
All the detail the modern rail enthusiast could require on the engineering problems underlying the development of these new trains and how they were, or are being, overcome. Illustrated with many photographs and diagrams, and including details of record runs, this second edition is even better value than the first.

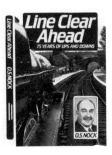

Line Clear Ahead
75 years of ups and downs
O.S. Nock
From top engineer and doyen of railway writers O.S. Nock, a personal, semi-autobiographical look back over 75 years of railway developments, journeys and personalities, illustrated with many of the author's personal photographs. Shows both how rail travel has, and has not, changed since before the First World War.

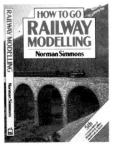

How To Go Railway Modelling
5th edition
Norman Simmons
Widely accepted as the 'bible' of the hobby, as tens of thousands of satisfied readers will attest, this is a complete introduction to scales, gauges, track, locos, stock, electrification, controllers, signalling, scenery and operating, with many valuable appendices.

Full catalogue available free of charge on request.

Paddington-Wolverhampton express, via Oxford, on Hatton bank: engine No 4938 Liddington Hall (R. Blenkinsop).